The Black Arcl

ROSE

By Jon Arnold

Published March 2016 by Obverse Books
Cover Design © Cody Schell
Text © Jon Arnold, 2016

Range Editor: Philip Purser-Hallard

Jon would like to thank:

Dave, for the goading.Geoff, Jim, Jon, Jonn, Blair, Stuart, Bryan, Steffan, Finn and Simon for helpful discussions.
John, Ian, Graeme, Robert, Bob, Paul, Jamie and Leslie and J.R. for helping me develop these ideas at length elsewhere.
Michael for being a confidant and sounding board, and tracking down documents at the right time.
Carolyn and Eddie for being tolerant when I needed to disappear to write.Mum and Dad, for incubating and nurturing a lifelong love of **Doctor Who** *and support throughout the process.*
Phil, for being the sympathetic and thorough editor every writer needs. And all involved in bringing **Doctor Who** *back in 2005.*

Dedicated to Vi, who'll never read it but would be eternally proud anyway.

CONTENTS

OVERVIEW

Serial Title: *Rose*

Writer: Russell T Davies

Director: Keith Boak

Original UK Transmission Date: 26 March 2005

Running Time: 44m 19s

UK Viewing Figures: 10.81 million

Regular cast: Christopher Eccleston (Doctor Who), Billie Piper (Rose Tyler)

Recurring Cast: Camille Coduri (Jackie Tyler), Noel Clarke (Mickey Smith)

Guest Cast: Mark Benton (Clive), Caroline (Elli Garnett), Clive's Son (Adam McCoy), Alan Ruscoe, Paul Kasey, David Sant, Elizabeth Fost, Helen Otway (Autons), Nicholas Briggs (Nestene Voice)

Antagonists: Nestene Consciousness, Autons

Sequels and Prequels: *Love and Monsters* (TV, 2006), *The Beast of Babylon* (ebook, 2013)

Responses:

'...a fabulous, imaginative, funny and sometimes frightening re-invention of the esteemed, if somewhat time ravaged, Time Lord.'

[Harry Venning, 'TV Review'. *The Stage*, 4 March 2005]

'Let's start with the negatives – and there are many. This is **Who** for the attention deficit disorder generation.'

[Stephen Brook, 'Carry on Doctor'. *The Guardian*, 9 March 2005]

SYNOPSIS

Locking up after an ordinary day of work, ordinary department store assistant **Rose Tyler** unexpectedly encounters menacing animated plastic mannequins – and **the Doctor**, who rescues her before blowing up the shop. He later follows her to the flat she shares with her mother **Jackie**, to claim an arm she kept from one of the dummies. Intrigued by the stranger, Rose seeks out **Clive**, a conspiracy theorist who has been gathering evidence of the Doctor's appearances over the past century.

While Rose is with Clive, her boyfriend **Mickey** is swallowed by a plastic rubbish bin. A replica Mickey takes Rose for pizza, to pump her for information about the Doctor. Their meal is interrupted by the Doctor himself, who again saves Rose from the murderous plastic duplicate, this time taking her inside the TARDIS. He explains that the living plastic beings are Autons, animated by **the Nestene Consciousness** in an attempt to colonise Earth after its own planets were destroyed in a war.

Following the signal animating the duplicate, the Doctor and Rose track the Consciousness to an underground chamber beneath the London Eye, where Mickey is being held. The Doctor has a vial of anti-plastic with which he intends to destroy the Consciousness if it refuses to leave Earth, but he is immobilised by the Autons. The Consciousness is alarmed to discover that the Doctor is a Time Lord, and involved in the war which made it homeless. While shop-window mannequins go on a murderous rampage across London, killing Clive and threatening Jackie, Rose draws on her junior-school gymnastics skills to free the Doctor, allowing him to fulfil his plan.

The Doctor offers Rose the opportunity to leave Mickey and travel with him in the TARDIS. Initially she declines, but on learning that it is a time machine as well as a spaceship, she accepts.

INTRODUCTION: 'D'YER WANNA COME WITH ME'?

Rose (2005) is the most radical episode ever broadcast under the title **Doctor Who**. It may not appear that way 10 years later, now that the changes it brought to the series are an integral part of the format; now that the 21st-century audience it lured in has become the dominant audience, an audience that didn't know they needed a Doctor until Eccleston, Tennant, Smith or Capaldi grabbed them by the hand and invited them on the trip of a lifetime; now that both BBC and ITV have attempted to clone the success of a Saturday night adventure series with the likes of **Merlin** (2008-12), **Primeval** (2007-11), **Robin Hood** (2006-09), **Demons** (2009) and **Atlantis** (2013-15); now that the show is a Saturday night and Christmas Day institution, having piled up mainstream TV and Hugo awards and, for one glorious week, been the most watched show in the country[1], the Doctor an integral part of the British cultural psyche once more.

This is the context of its triumph. The series had ended its original BBC run just over 15 years earlier, striking a notably optimistic and imaginative note with a speech about 'people made of smoke and

---

[1] For the finale of the fourth series, *Journey's End* (2008). The previous week's *The Stolen Earth* (2008) was only beaten by the final of the Euro 2008 football tournament, and the Christmas Day episodes *The Christmas Invasion* (2005), *Voyage of the Damned* (2007) and *A Christmas Carol* (2010) were second to 'festive' episodes of **EastEnders** (1985-).

cities made of song'[2]. The show had had a troubled existence since the mid-1980s, when Michael Grade, a man unsympathetic to science fiction in general and **Doctor Who** in particular, had attempted to cancel it. It survived that first attempt and even rediscovered an imaginative creative approach towards the end of its original run. Ultimately, though, it was always doomed: under budgeted and deliberately scheduled in a graveyard slot opposite the most popular show of the time, **Coronation Street** (1960-).

It's easy to see the show as retreating into the cult television ghetto for the next decade, but this is not quite true. It thrived away from the spotlight, maintaining a robust existence in audios, novels and a monthly comic strip in *Doctor Who Magazine*, all of which maintained healthy sales even without the parent show. There were also two contributions to charity telethons (*Dimensions In Time* for Children In Need in 1993 and *The Curse of Fatal Death* for Comic Relief in 1999), and an attempt to launch **Doctor Who** as a US co-production. Both telethon contributions treated the show as something of a nostalgia piece: *Dimensions In Time* celebrated the show's 30th anniversary with appearances by every living Doctor and a seemingly random jumble of companions, and *The Curse of Fatal Death* was an affectionate parody. Only the TV movie, *Doctor Who* (1996) was a serious attempt to relaunch the show. It garnered respectable ratings in the UK, gaining more than nine million viewers on a warm May bank holiday against ITV's popular Victorian medical drama **Bramwell** (1995-98).

---

[2] *Survival* episode 3, broadcast 6 December 1989. The irony of the final broadcast serial's title has not been lost on fans.

However, the show going to a series depended on US ratings, and poor creative decisions and unfavourable scheduling in the US against a significant episode of **Roseanne** (1988-97) and an NBA playoff game featuring Michael Jordan, the most popular sports star of the decade, meant that it was doomed before it had even been broadcast on UK television[3]. Even the range of novels published by BBC Books in the wake of the movie disappointed; launched with adverts in the national media, they were soon selling almost exclusively to the same fans who had bought the previous ranges from Virgin Publishing. The start of the Big Finish audios, seemingly catering mainly for fans nostalgic for **Doctor Who** as it used to be, merely reinforced the impression that the show's appeal had contracted to that slowly declining core audience.

And then, on 26 September 2003, two months before the show's 40th anniversary, the BBC announced that **Doctor Who** would return. Only three facts were revealed in that initial press release; that Russell T Davies would be writing the show, that it would be made by BBC Wales and that the executive producers would be Davies, Mal Young and the Head of Drama for BBC Wales, Julie Gardner. The press release emphasised that this was a resurrection, with Young referring to it as 'truly iconic' and Davies recalling 'hiding behind the sofa'. Yet Davies was also keen to emphasise that this would be a modern take on the series:

> 'The new series will be fun, exciting, contemporary and scary... I'm aiming to write a full-blooded drama which

---

[3] *Doctor Who* was broadcast on 14 May in the United States and 27 May in the UK.

embraces the **Doctor Who** heritage, at the same time as introducing the character to a modern audience.'[4]

Quietly hidden away, amongst notes that there was no detail as to budgets, number or length of episodes or scheduling, was the declaration that this would be a family show. This was something that the show had moved away from in the 1980s for several reasons: the 1982 shift to an early evening timeslot, an increasing tendency to play to the nascent fan audience which led to an emphasis on the show's history, and 1982-86 script editor Eric Saward's fascination with violence and conflict. Incidents such as melted faces in *Resurrection of the Daleks* (1984), the infamous scene where Lytton's hands are bloodily crushed in *Attack of the Cybermen* (1985) or Oscar Botcherby being stabbed in the stomach in *The Two Doctors* (1985) were always liable to alienate a substantial portion of any family audience. The new series would get back to that core aim that had been a major part of the conception of the show in 1963[5].

There was a slow but regular drip of news over the next nine months – former pop star Billie Piper would be the companion, Christopher Eccleston would play the Doctor, Davies would be joined in writing that first series by Mark Gatiss, Rob Shearman, Paul Cornell and Steven Moffat, fans who had carved out a career as successful writers. And the show was to attract a high calibre of

---

[4] 'Doctor Who Returns to BBC One'.

[5] Webber, C E, 'Concept Notes for New SF Drama'. This internal BBC memo does not deal with **Doctor Who** directly, but outlines the desire for a Saturday night science fiction TV series with characters designed to appeal to different sections of the audience.

guest star – Zoe Wanamaker, Simon Callow, Penelope Wilton, Simon Pegg and Richard Wilson would all appear in the first season. **Doctor Who** film crews became a common sight around Newport and Cardiff in 2004 and 2005; this writer was delighted to discover that the studios for the first two series were unexpectedly located five minutes from his house and even to see Eccleston and Piper rehearsing when walking past it on his way home from work. A 30-second trailer aired on 1 January 2005, comprising the initial zoom from *Rose*, dialogue from the episode[6], a section of the title sequence and the TARDIS dematerialising. This was followed in the weeks leading up to transmission by a national billboard poster campaign, a public launch and two more trailers. The main one saw Eccleston's Doctor running down a corridor away from a fireball, intercut with a scene of him on the TARDIS set asking viewers if they want to come with him, telling them of delights to come and promising the trip of a lifetime. The second focussed on Piper's Rose, detailing her dilemma of whether to stay at home with her mum, her boyfriend and her job or chuck it all in for danger, monsters and life or death. Provocatively she ended by asking the viewers what they thought. It sought to offer something for fans of spectacle and those who simply liked a good drama. The message was clear: this was a series which openly invited viewers in without prejudice, which wanted to give them every opportunity to become hooked on it.

---

[6] The dialogue is taken from the Doctor and Rose's first meeting, with the Doctor introducing himself, asking Rose's name and then telling her to run for her life.

13

On 26 March 2005 **Doctor Who** came back. And everything changed.

CHAPTER 1: 'DID I MENTION IT ALSO TRAVELS IN TIME?'

'If the moment the opening titles are over you go into a Scene One that's set on a purple planet with three moons, and some man in a cloak is making a villainous death threat, then the audience would switch off in their millions.'

[Russell T Davies][7]

In the 21st century superheroes began to rule mainstream cinema; masked crimefighters now dominate the big budget releases as soldiers and cowboys once ruled them. Few of these films are designed as one-offs; they are either part of a larger design or the first in a designated franchise, and sometimes both. Unlike those earlier genres, though, the makers of these films seem compelled to present an origin story for the hero to begin with, detailing how they became the hero and decided on their particular method of battling evil. Batman, Spider-man, Superman, Iron Man, Green Lantern, the Hulk… before viewers have been able to embark on adventures with these heroes they have had to dutifully sit through an explanation of each hero's journey with their initial adventure, a trend dating back to Richard Donner's *Superman: The Movie* (1978).

Even when audiences might be assumed to be familiar with the character's origins, fresh cinematic iterations have largely stuck to repeating the story and insisting on going over old ground –

---

[7] Various, 'We're Gonna Be Bigger Than Star Wars!'. Doctor Who Magazine (DWM) #279, p10.

Superman, Spider-Man, the Hulk and the Fantastic Four have all had their origins told more than once. As audiences we can't be asked to accept that heroes are possible, instead we have to have it carefully explained to us just why such heroes exist, even if the story is familiar. We are asked to buy into the mythology immediately. We are being told these people are heroes, and having their powers and their world explained to us.

It is an approach which leaves little direction for sequels to go in – if we know these characters and their background so thoroughly by the end of the first movie, why should we come back for more, particularly in an age where spectacle is relatively cheap? The essential myth of the hero has been compressed into their first story. The modern superhero movie formulaically clings to the hero's journey as outlined by Joseph Campbell: the call to adventure, the road of trials, the boon, the return to the ordinary world and the application of their boon before the end credits have rolled. Their essential story has fundamentally been told, and all that is left to explore is variations on a theme.

It's notable that **Doctor Who**, arguably the most successful cultural revival of the 21st century, takes almost exactly the opposite approach.

Doctor Who has had three attempts at introducing itself to a new audience; in 1963 with 'An Unearthly Child' (*An Unearthly Child* episode 1), in 1996 with the Fox TV movie and in 2005 with *Rose*. Other stories have marked shifts in format but came after gaps measured in months rather than years. These three stories were all intended to introduce **Doctor Who** to audiences unfamiliar with the show. 'An Unearthly Child' set up an entirely new series; the TV movie sought to introduce **Doctor Who** to a mainstream US audience and *Rose* looked to appeal to a mainstream audience, a large number of whom would have an at best passing familiarity with the show thanks to its being largely relegated to nostalgic repeats, books and audios for 16 years. Where 'An Unearthly Child' and the TV movie take diametrically different approaches in trying to find an audience, *Rose* is informed by both of them, learning from the successes and failures of both.

As an introduction 'An Unearthly Child' is a marvel of economy. After an opening shot which presents an incongruous humming police box in a junkyard, the first half is told in flashback, with two teachers discussing a pupil with knowledge that is in some ways strangely advanced but lacking in more basic ways. That peculair pupil, the unearthly child, is the hook that brings them to the junkyard where they find their pupil's grandfather and his bigger-on-the-inside ship which travels in time and space.

The episode goes out of its way to render the lead character as blank a canvas as possible – indeed, when the episode was re-recorded a specific explanation of his origin was removed. No longer from the 49th century[8], he is simply a wanderer in the fourth dimension[9]. The Doctor's background is no more than a sketched-in detail to provide a reason for him to be away from his home in this machine. Partly this is undoubtedly so as not to cut off possibilities for writers of future stories, but mainly because this is not an area the show is particularly interested in at this point. It's

---

[8] Pilot episode (1963), included on the *An Unearthly Child* DVD release (2006).
[9] 'An Unearthly Child' (*An Unearthly Child* episode 1, 1963).

an adventure series exploring strange, futuristic worlds and Earth history; the Doctor's background is of no interest, as the show is not about him but about the worlds and civilisations they visit. He's essentially a walking narrative device to catalyse an anthology of stories of almost infinite scope. The point of this episode is to get Ian and Barbara into the TARDIS and for them to join the Doctor and Susan in their journeys, to get a couple of everyman characters journeying in time and space. What we are told is just enough to intrigue, to render the Doctor a little stranger than his companions, and to give us an idea of the Doctor and Susan's capabilities.

The motivation which subsequently drives the story in these early episodes is Ian and Barbara's quest to return to the London of 1963, not to uncover or even investigate the mystery of the Doctor. Indeed, there is precious little interest in the Doctor's origins throughout the William Hartnell era, bar a description of the environment of his home planet in *The Sensorites* (1964), and even through the Patrick Troughton era we get little but hints (such as a reference to the Doctor's family in *The Tomb of the Cybermen* (1967)) before the revelation in *The War Games* (1969) of the Doctor's people and of why he's wandering the universe. This is a series which remains light on its feet for the first six years, before the continuity references encrust on it like barnacles and fans begin to build a history for the main character and his people. What matters is that within 25 minutes a bizarre concept – an old man who lives in a police box which can go anywhere in time and space – has been rendered dramatically plausible to the audience and a story has been built around it.

It would be difficult to take a similarly light approach over 40 years after that first episode – throwing away the accumulated history completely would unnecessarily alienate the core audience of fans that already existed, and limit the use of the series' icons which may have had some wider recognition. But equally it would be a mistake to pitch a new audience straight into a world of arcane references and character history; it would probably alienate them if it were thrown at them at once. This was the mistake made by the TV movie of 1996; its makers relied too much on the show's name and mythology for appeal.

The viewer of *Doctor Who* (1996) is thrown into not so much a deep end as an ocean of history. The Master and the Daleks are introduced before the opening credits and the concepts of regeneration, TARDISes and the Eye of Harmony follow in short order. There is no thought to holding back any major elements for the series; the icons of **Doctor Who** are all introduced in this intended pilot. Rather than recreate the sense of intrigue that worked in 1963, the producers seemed to have decided what's cool about **Doctor Who** is the mythology, and tried to wow the audience with this from the first scene. This didn't appear to be a particular problem for British viewers, where there was still a large section of the audience familiar with the show – it attracted a healthy 9.1 million viewers on a Bank Holiday[10] – but given that the fate of this version of the show depended on how well it did in the USA, this continuity overload immediately hobbled its appeal.

Coupled with a confused script which ended up treating time travel as an illogical plot cheat, it's a poor introduction to the show,

---

[10] Pixley, Andrew, 'DWM Archive: Doctor Who – The Movie'. DWM Special Edition: *The Complete Eighth Doctor*, p69.

something the programme's 1970s producer Barry Letts and script editor Terrance Dicks were none too shy about stating after watching it[11]. Whilst its failure to lead to a series is also down to wider issues such as scheduling against a narratively important episode of **Roseanne** and production values which look merely reasonable for the time, the approach does nothing to welcome new viewers, seeking to impress them with a tour of **Doctor Who**. It renders **Doctor Who** as a cultural artefact to be admired, rather than something engaged with.

Rose essentially learns the positive lessons from 'An Unearthly Child' and what to avoid from *Doctor Who* (1996). The first lesson is clear from the episode title; this is Rose's story, told from her point of view. Unlike the TV movie's creators, Davies does not make the assumption that the Doctor is interesting in his own right; rather he uses the 45 minutes of *Rose* to set him up as an intriguing figure and works, via Rose, to make him someone the audience wishes to know more about. This mirrors how the production team of 1963 chose to introduce the Doctor, initially familiarising us with point-of-view characters to represent normality, and then through the investigation of a series of strange events, having the unreality of the Doctor's universe intrude upon that normality.

The baseline level these introductory episodes choose for 'normality' is informative about the 20th- and 21st- century versions of the series (and indeed about Russell T Davies's views).

---

[11] '...that indigestible mish mash...' (Letts, Barry, *Who & Me*, p65); '...a weird, fantastic adventure, full of improbable, illogical events' (Dicks, Terrance, *The Eight Doctors* p1).

Ian and Barbara are steadfastly middle-class teachers, grounding the initial series in a middle-class milieu. Choosing them as a viewpoint is almost a caricature of the image of the 1960s' BBC as a middle-class organisation seeking to educate viewers didactically. *Doctor Who* (1996) attempts to use Grace as the viewpoint character, but this is fatally flawed as her interests and profession are not something the majority of viewers could relate to (she's a surgeon who listens to opera and sits on boards of major scientific projects). It tries to overcome this by giving her a messy personal life, but the early emphasis on her occupation and interest already means it's difficult for the character to elicit audience empathy.

Rose, by contrast to Ian, Barbara or Grace, is a working-class shop assistant. This is a key point of Davies's version of **Doctor Who**. Our viewpoint character, the one who introduces us to the Doctor, is a young girl from a council estate stuck in the twin drudgeries of a retail job and a comfortable but sparkless relationship, drifting through life and wasting any potential. This version of **Doctor Who** is seeking to avoid exclusively reflecting concerns which might be perceived as middle-class, such as science and literature, but is looking to reflect the democratic power of television as a mass medium; one which is capable of reaching across divides of class, race and gender by focussing on human concerns.

With the series' position at the heart of the Saturday night schedule it is arguably a necessity to take this approach, giving the viewpoint character as wide an appeal as possible to draw in viewers with little knowledge or prior interest in the series. 'An Unearthly Child' was broadcast in an era of two channels (and even then a channel could only be changed manually, involving not only thought but effort) so could afford a slow burn, but *Rose* had to fight for an audience against hundreds of channels and hold the attention of viewers who could change the channel with barely a second thought.

In practice this means that Rose is constantly seeking to dazzle viewers; to hook them and bring them back next week. 'An Unearthly Child' can afford to be far more sedate in pace and content than Rose – there are no explosions, no explicit aliens, simply the marvel of the first glimpse of the TARDIS interior and the sequence of the TARDIS in flight. The hook is in the odd ideas at the heart of the story. Rose, by contrast, sees shop window dummies coming to life and a department store blown up inside the first 10 minutes.

Both versions of the show are made to fill a perceived gap in early Saturday evening television, and the difference in pacing is illustrative of how much Saturday evening television changed over decades[12]. Where 'An Unearthly Child' relies mainly on dialogue and acting, Rose deliberately dazzles with special effects, explosions, alien invasion set-pieces and computer-generated imagery (CGI), seeking to augment intrigue with spectacle. The point is clearly being made that this is no longer a series where budgetary limitations are a regular and obvious problem[13]. This is

---

[12] It's worth noting that the TV movie is a different animal again, deliberately not pitched towards the family audience but a more adult one; something confirmed by its evening scheduling in both the UK and USA.

[13] Although on **Newsnight Review** prior to Rose's broadcast (18 March 2005) Bonnie Greer, an American TV critic, dismissed the episode as looking 'really cheap' compared to other science fiction,

one of the big myths *Rose* seeks to demolish, the perception of the show as one of wobbly sets and bubble-wrap monsters. Russell T Davies, painfully aware of that reputation for cheapness, makes visual spectacle a hallmark of his tenure; the end of the world, the demolition of London landmarks and armies of Daleks will follow by the end of the season. The increasingly flamboyant spectacles of his season finales can be seen as not only laying the ghost of the Myrka[14] but dismembering its corpse and salting the earth.

Whilst this drive for spectacle smooths over the qualms of older audience members, it also provides an opportunity to forge a new reputation to attract the mass audience that has grown up in the 16 years where **Doctor Who** has been restricted to one new episode and a couple of charity sketches. There may be an audience out there who might watch out of nostalgia, but there is also a younger audience with no expectations of what an episode of **Doctor Who** might look like, who were not familiar with the old series. By the time of *Rose*'s broadcast, even the last terrestrial repeat had been five years earlier[15]; **Doctor Who** was now a show viewers had to actively look for on satellite channels or in books, DVDs or CDs, slipping slowly into the cosy territory of nostalgia. Audience research conducted by BBC Worldwide prior to *Rose*'s

---

with John Carey agreeing by arguing that cheapness was 'part of the appeal'.

[14] The notorious 'pantomime horse' dinosaur from *Warriors of the Deep* (1984).

[15] 'Airdates in the UK (BBC Repeats)', BroaDWcast.

broadcast revealed no great appetite for the return of the series[16]. This chance was there to be radical with the show's format, to bring a whole new audience to it. Indeed, this was crucial to the success of the revived show.

This is where the role of companion as audience identification figure was vital. Rose Tyler is not simply a viewpoint character; she is also a direct avatar for the new viewer. The mundanity of her daily routine is quickly established in an early montage – the alarm clock, the rush to get ready, the commute to a job in a department store and meeting her boyfriend on her lunch break. We even see Rose and Mickey eating chips, a shorthand for the normality of everyday life that will be repeated in *The End of the World* and *The Parting of the Ways* (both 2005). And at the end of her working day she has collected the lottery money to give to Wilson the electrician, who presumably runs the syndicate. The initial montage bombards us with signifiers of the everyday, and makes it clear that, although there are moments of dissatisfaction, this isn't an entirely joyless existence. It's a representation of an ordinary, working-class life; estates, chips and the tiny hope of escape offered by the lottery.

Of course, Rose hits an entirely different type of jackpot by being involved in her lottery syndicate. Whilst collecting the money she is confronted by the dummies in the shop coming to life late at night; this is terrifying as she's alone in a dimly-lit shop basement. Her ordinary life has been intruded upon by the extraordinary – this is

---

[16] Research cited by Jane Tranter and Julie Gardner in Scott, Cavan, 'The Way Back Part One: Bring Me To Life'. DWM #463, p23.

something unexpected and strange, deliberately unsettling. However, it is something she can vaguely frame in terms of her experience. The world of the Doctor is grounded in the familiar and rendered accessible to an audience unfamiliar with the concepts underlying the series.

By contrast to Rose representing the new audience, the old fan audience, those already familiar with the Doctor, are more closely represented by Clive. In many respects it's a gently cruel portrayal. Clive is presented as something of an obsessive, an oddball maintaining a website about the Doctor, a character at this point only of interest to a tiny number of people. It's an obsession even his family despair of, his son calling Rose 'one of your nutters'. As a small dig his wife is amazed when Rose visits, 'She? She's read a website about the Doctor and she's a she?' And in a typically British touch Clive runs his website and keeps his material on the Doctor in his shed (described as his 'den' in the script, the language reflecting his nature as an overgrown child)[17]. Clive is a fairly obvious caricature of existing **Doctor Who** fandom of the time; predominantly male, often socially awkward and closeting their obsession away from the rest of the world[18]. It's a pleasant twist

---

[17] Davies, Russell T, et al, *Doctor Who: The Shooting Scripts*, p27.

[18] Doctor Who has always had a significant non-heterosexual following; in that sense parallels to gay men coming out of the closet are obvious and have been drawn many times over the years, including in the uncredited 'Telling Your Boyfriend' in Paul Cornell's 1997 collection of fanzine writing *Licence Denied* and Paul Magrs's 2010 novel *The Diary of a Dr. Who Addict*. The fan phrase coined for declaring your love of the show to non-fan friends or significant others was 'coming out of the TARDIS'.

that Clive's obsession has not driven a wedge between him and the rest of the human race, but instead it's the quirk of a family man. While much of what we see of Clive might be thought of as a caricature of fans, it's pleasant to see it acknowledged that fans can and do lead what we think of as conventional lives, and find a reasonably compassionate portrayal here, rather than the stereotypical anorak-wearing nutter of cheap 90s comedy routines.

That said, Clive does meet a Darwinian fate – whereas Rose (and the new audience)[19] help save the day and go off adventuring with the Doctor, Clive, the avatar for the old audience, gets shot in the face for his troubles. The old makes way for the new. In narrative terms this can be read as reflecting their contrasting fannish approaches – Rose and Clive both get exactly what they expect from their encounters with the Doctor's world. Rose embraces the

---

[19] Rose was deliberately designed to show that an interest in the Doctor was not exclusively the province of these closeted males (indeed it never was: despite fandom being dominated by men there were female novelists for the Virgin and BBC **Doctor Who** novel ranges such as Kate Orman, Mags L Halliday and Lloyd Rose, and the *Doctor Who Magazine* column 'The Life and Times of Jackie Jenkins'). The changed nature of fandom since 2005 indicates that this was successful, with the series able to sustain a magazine aimed at children (**Doctor Who Adventures**, 2006-) and an increased female presence in fandom, as exemplified by Mad Norwegian's **Geek Girl Chronicles** series, feminist fanzines such as *The Terrible Zodin*, the all-female podcast *Verity* and fan-fiction websites such as *A Teaspoon and an Open Mind*. The series itself has explicitly acknowledged the increased prominence of fangirls with the recurring character of Osgood, introduced in *The Day of the Doctor* (2013).

adventure of the Doctor's world, seeing the joy of his existence. She actively helps him, engaging with his adventures, and ends up not only surviving but invited into the TARDIS for further adventures. Clive, by contrast, has built the Doctor up into a strange and terrible figure always accompanied by death, and ends up getting exactly what he expected too[20].

This can be seen as a deliberate wooing of the general audience; that the emphasis of this series will be on life and adventure – the thrilling 'now' of the Doctor's adventures rather than the darker death and angst of the past. History and mythology are cast off, to be discovered if the new audience is interested but irrelevant to enjoying the current adventures.

This is further demonstrated by the elements of the past that Davies chooses to use in *Rose*. The most obvious of these is the Doctor himself. With the episode being told from Rose's viewpoint, the viewer is privy only to the same information Rose is. By the end

---

[20] Clive's view of the Doctor is similar to one espoused by Davies in the DWM 'We're Gonna Be Bigger Than Star Wars' article. This perspective of a darker Doctor may be a further parallel to the existing fan audience. Influenced by revisionist comic work such as Frank Miller's **Batman** comic *The Dark Knight Returns* and works by the likes of Alan Moore, Neil Gaiman and Grant Morrison, the writers of **Doctor Who** novels in the 1990s had built on hints in stories such as *Remembrance of the Daleks* (1988), *Ghost Light* (1989) and *The Curse of Fenric* (1989) to frame the Doctor as a dark character weighted down by the consequences of his adventures. Paul Cornell's 1991 novel *Timewyrm: Revelation* and Ben Aaronovitch's *Remembrance of the Daleks* script and novelisation are the key texts here.

of the story we have been told little more than we need to know to set up the series: the Doctor is an alien who travels in time and space in his TARDIS, and has fought in a war. These are the only elements Davies considers essential to his version of **Doctor Who**, the only fundamental elements needed to tell a **Doctor Who** story. Again, this is worth comparing to the background information we get in 'An Unearthly Child' – the Doctor and Susan are 'wanderers in the fourth dimension', 'exiles' and '...cut off from [their] own planet'.

The only acknowledgement of the information about the Doctor accumulated from 1963 to 2005 is his alien nature, and even this is kept as vague as possible, a detail to be expanded upon at a later date. The only fresh mythology we get about the Doctor (bar small details such as his presence at the Kennedy assassination, the launch of the *Titanic* and the 1883 explosion of Krakatoa) is that small tantalising hint that he has fought in a war, referred to here as 'the war'. This only emerges as an incidental detail in the final showdown with the Nestene Consciousness, and is left dangling as a hint for the future[21]. The effect of this for new viewers is to prioritise the mysterious war as the series' primary mythological hook; something they can latch on to as one of the few details presented regarding the Doctor's past. Again, the emphasis is on intrigue rather than explanation, with Davies very conscious that he needs to hook viewers for an ongoing series.

---

[21] The final scene also indicates that this is a war which destroys worlds: a hint of the epic.

This approach can be seen later, when *Rose*'s fictional portrait of the development of a new fandom is completed in the second season story *Love & Monsters* (2006) with the character of Elton Pope. This story is explicitly a love letter to fandom and the power of fan communities, but is very much an embracing of a new fandom rather than the older one. Elton's encounters with the Doctor either involve figures familiar only to those only watching since *Rose* — Autons, the fake spaceship from *Aliens of London* (2005), the Sycorax from *The Christmas Invasion* (2005), the 10th Doctor and the Tylers — or entirely new creatures (the Hoix and an Elemental Shade from the Howling Halls). Whilst this episode is about fans and the way they interact with the objects of their affection, Davies never loses sight of the fact that this is a show made for a mass audience; the new aliens are integral to the story and the inclusions from the past are ones that are known to the new viewer. Davies eventually includes references to stories which predate *Rose*, but only in places where they will not affect the plot or a casual viewer's enjoyment[22].

The other significant element from the Doctor's past that Davies chooses to include in *Rose* is the Autons. With their last appearance in *Terror of the Autons* (1971) being 34 years earlier, they will generally only be recalled by fans and older viewers with long memories (and perhaps those who few who watched the 1999

---

[22] These include such scenes as the **Weakest Link** sequence in *Bad Wolf* (2015) referencing *The Web Planet* (1965), Sarah Jane's face-off with Rose about who's faced better monsters in *School Reunion* (2006), and the later appearance of the Macra from *The Macra Terror* (1967) in *Gridlock* (2007).

29

BBC2 repeat of *Spearhead from Space* (1970)). That Davies chooses to use these relatively obscure aliens ahead of more obvious candidates such as the Daleks or Cybermen is indicative of his approach to **Doctor Who** and its mythology: it's a toybox for him to tell the stories he wants to tell, rather than the point of a storytelling exercise.

The Autons are used specifically for their ability to pass for human at a quick glance, and their modus operandi involving the disturbance of a mundane domestic setting. They are the most logical choice from **Doctor Who**'s gallery of monsters to allow a shop assistant to become involved in an alien invasion. Rose works in a department store, and the shop window dummies coming to life is unsettling and odd; a place of domesticity suddenly rendered shockingly alien. A Dalek gliding in might be shocking, but its shape and obvious alienness simply wouldn't give the scene in Henrik's basement such an unsettling feel. It would be difficult to rationalise in the way Rose attempts to rationalise it during her first encounter with the Doctor; it would hit Rose and the viewers with the undeniably alien immediately and would demand an explanation as to why it was hiding in a department store basement. Hostile dummies naturally have a reason to be in a department store; actual explanations are not particularly important when what matters is the Doctor and Rose meeting, and can be deferred for later. In plot terms all that is needed is generic alien invaders, but the Autons combine with Rose working in a shop to provide a perfect mechanism to involve her in an alien invasion.

Essentially, the choice of the Autons allows Davies to tell his story; they have been carefully selected as their abilities reassure the fans that this is the same series. For all that the old audience is symbolically killed off during the show, those old viewers who are willing to embrace the series in the same way as the new viewers are equally welcome. It's a regeneration rather than a complete rebirth.

Ultimately, the initial attitude of the 21st-century series to its past is a wise one. Whilst long-term fans are rewarded by the appearance of the Autons and the Nestene Consciousness, these are treated in a way which will not distract viewers from the more important elements of the story: Rose and the Doctor getting together, and the establishment of new myths for a new century.

Under the aegis of John Nathan-Turner and Eric Saward in the 1980s, the series had become almost obsessed with its past, publicising its 20th season with the boast that each story contained an element from the Doctor's past[23]. From *Earthshock* (1982) onwards there is a run of 10 stories which feature characters and monsters from the show's past (beyond the TARDIS and the series regulars). Between the Peter Davison and Colin Baker era only nine stories do not feature such elements[24]. Although the show's decline in ratings over this period is caused by a complex set of circumstances, the constant reappearance of old villains and the perceived need to explain their appearance cannot have appealed

---

[23] Howe, David J and Walker, Stephen James, *Doctor Who: The Television Companion*, p423.

[24] These are *Four to Doomsday, Kinda, Black Orchid* (all 1982), *The Awakening, Frontios, The Caves of Androzani, The Twin Dilemma* (all 1984), *Vengeance on Varos* and *Timelash* (both 1985) Of these nine stories, four were commissioned prior to Saward taking over as script editor.

to the casual viewer; perhaps the notorious line in *Time-Flight* (1982), 'So you escaped from Castrovalva', which simply skates over the Master's reappearance, is a wiser course of action than it appears. The Master's fate at the end of the previous story is brushed over and the writer can proceed with the story he is telling. **Doctor Who** was designed as mass entertainment and its survival for 26 years depended to a large degree on its ability to adapt to changing times. But in the 1980s it began to look backwards, to eat itself. Even under Andrew Cartmel's script editorship six of the 12 Sylvester McCoy stories feature returning characters and monsters[25]. The show roots itself in the past throughout this decade, something continued by *Doctor Who* (1996).

Rose seeks to redress this balance: the Autons, the element from the show's past, are not explained in greater depth than the story requires – they control plastic and they are invading because their feeding grounds were destroyed in a war. Their previous invasions of Earth are not mentioned, nor explained. The Doctor is simply an alien who can travel in time and space in a police box and recently fought in the same war[26]. Davies's script strips the show down to its

---

[25] Past elements appear in *Time and the Rani* (1987) (the Rani), *Dragonfire* (1987) (Sabalom Glitz), *Remembrance of the Daleks* (Daleks), *Silver Nemesis* (1987) (Cybermen), *Battlefield* (1989) (Brigadier Lethbridge-Stewart and UNIT) and *Survival* (1989) (the Master). *Time and the Rani*, McCoy's debut, was commissioned by John Nathan-Turner in the interregnum between Saward's resignation and Cartmel's hiring.
[26] According to Davies in *Rose*'s DVD commentary, the Doctor is named as a Time Lord in the Nestene Consciousness's dialogue;

basics, tantalises with a few sketchy details and roots the series in the more character-led environment of 21st-century UK television drama. To attempt to establish the show in the hearts and minds of a new generation, Davies gives us just enough to provide the Doctor with an intriguing side. He wants the audience to join the Doctor's travels because the Doctor is interesting, not because the places he's been and the people and creatures he's met are fascinating. He sells the **now** of the show with this initial episode, not a tour of the show's past. His interest as a writer, and therefore ours as viewers, is in the characters of the Doctor and Rose.

Davies's conception of **Doctor Who** as character-based drama is essentially a brand-new product placed in familiar packaging. And in applying this he proves **Doctor Who**'s credentials as what Steven Moffat more recently described as 'a television predator designed to survive any environment because you can replace absolutely everybody.'[27] The only essentials are the Doctor and his time machine (although theoretically there's no reason why even the police box cannot be replaced)[28]; everything else – companions,

---

however this has been so heavily processed and treated it is near indecipherable without the aid of subtitles or prior knowledge.

[27] Vivarelli, Nick, 'Lucca Comics: Doctor Who Showrunner Steven Moffat on Why the Reboot Is a Global Hit'.

[28] Several stories have not featured the TARDIS: *The Silurians* (1970), *The Sontaran Experiment* (1975), *Genesis of the Daleks* (1975), and *Midnight* (2008). *Heaven Sent* (2015) only features an imagined version. On other occasions it has been replaced or transformed – for instance it becomes invisible in *The Invasion* (1968); is partially destroyed in *Frontios*; has its chameleon circuit restored briefly in *Attack of the Cybermen*; and becomes the heart

writers, producers, story lengths – can be changed. The success of this approach not only secures **Doctor Who**'s immediate future, but, in demonstrating the absolute flexibility of its format, also its long-term one. Rather than the full story, this is the first step of a new journey for its hero.

---

of the Master's Paradox machine in *The Sound of Drums* (2007). It is essentially as much a narrative convenience as the sonic screwdriver; a simple means of transporting the Doctor and his companions between stories. It is not necessarily needed for any individual story, but the narrative ease with which it facilitates transport between locations is essential to the series itself.

CHAPTER 2: 'I'M THE DOCTOR, BY THE WAY'

'So, as a writer, I'm saying now: the Doctor I am writing is the same man who also fought the Drahvins, the Macra, the Axons, the Wirrn, the Tereleptils, the Borad, the Bannermen, and then the Master in San Francisco on New Year's Eve 1999. One man, nine faces.'

[Russell T Davies][29]

In retrospect the most important line in the initial press release for *Rose* was the one which concisely outlined Russell T Davies's vision: that it would be a full-blooded drama which embraced **Doctor Who**'s heritage. This constituted an immediate, fundamental change to the show's format, a shift from the show's enduring conception as an 'adventure series'[30] which signalled that Davies's version would be different from anything that had gone before and meant a change in the writing of the lead character.

For much of the 20th century run of the show, the Doctor was largely an eccentrically-dressed plot function, reliant on the charm and skills of the actor playing him, unchanging in nature. This was a consequence of the series' roots in serial TV of the 1960s. The ongoing series of those decades, the likes of **Dixon of Dock Green** (1955-76) or **The Avengers** (1961-69), essentially reset the characters at the end of each story so that they could return in a

---

[29] Russell T Davies, 'Production Notes #4: Think of A Number'. DWM #344.

[30] The show's original *Radio Times* description was 'an adventure in space and time', a description which remained until episode 10 of *The War Games* (1969).

similarly-structured story the next week. If any of the main characters underwent a significant change in personality then the series format would be changed. For that reason the Doctor's character remains essentially the same over the course of the first twenty-six seasons, despite traumas such as abandoning his granddaughter, seeing companions die, being exiled to Earth with his mind tampered with and witnessing a parallel Earth being destroyed[31]. There were minor references to these events but the main character essentially lived in an eternal now without major emotional consequences, typified by his abrupt abandonment of Sarah Jane in *The Hand of Fear* (1976) or dismissing the death of Adric in short order[32].

The only major change in the way the series used the Doctor came in 1966, under Producer Innes Lloyd and Script Editor Gerry Davis[33]. When they arrived the Doctor's role was that of an explorer; this was very much tied in with the educational aspect of the original series' brief. Stories generally alternated between visits to strange new worlds and showing periods of Earth history, with the explorative nature demonstrated by the structure of the stories. The first episode of each story is given over to establishing and presenting the world in which the serial occurs; that exploration of

---

[31] In *The Dalek Invasion of Earth* (1964), *The Daleks' Master Plan* (1965-66), *Spearhead from Space* and *Inferno* (1970) respectively.

[32] Adric's death, presented and played as a major trauma at *Earthshock*'s climax, was dealt with in one scene in the opening episode of *Time-Flight*.

[33] For some of the ways in which Lloyd and Davis transformed **Doctor Who**'s formula, see James Cooray Smith, *The Black Archive #2: The Massacre*.

36

the environment being visited is as important as the plot. What Lloyd and Davis did was to reshape the series in line with the most successful aspect of the show: the pulp science fiction element. Rather than entering situations which required investigation and thoughtful navigation (and where often the leads only wished to escape with their lives intact) the Doctor became a battler of monsters and foiler of invasions. This initially entailed several onscreen changes, such as the inherited companions being written out in favour of more obviously contemporary characters, and individual episode titles being dispensed with in favour of an umbrella title for each story. The final change, with William Hartnell being physically unsuited for the role of action hero, was to change the lead actor. With Patrick Troughton taking over, the metamorphosis of the show to something more straightforward was complete.

This general format would serve the show well for the remainder of its 20th-century run; each story is very much the Doctor battling clearly hostile monsters[34]. The series fundamentally became an action series; an anthology of science fiction stories linked by the main characters. The Doctor's character did not fundamentally alter after 1966, no matter the changes of face, exile to Earth or emotional departure of companions. The Doctor was practically guaranteed to do the right thing: the stranger who'd ride into town, put right what was wrong and quietly ride off into the sunset with the job done. He was a plot function with idiosyncrasies. Only

---

[34] Even *Black Orchid*, the only post-1966 story with no SF elements bar the Doctor and his companions, has a disfigured antagonist who's physically essentially a monster.

the final BBC script editor of the 20th century, Andrew Cartmel, played with the format by having the Doctor actively set up his adventures in advance. Even then, the character was fundamentally the same, to the point where the four adventures of the final two series were interchangeable in the schedules bar minor continuity glitches[35].

This lack of character development was not a viable option for the show's 21st-century return. The barely-connected series of adventures was out of fashion; since the series had been off the air for much of the 1990s it had become fashionable to introduce ongoing plot and character elements into drama shows. **The X-Files** (1993-2002, 2016-) had an ongoing conspiracy arc; **Babylon 5** (1993-98) had a planned five-year plot; and, most importantly, shows such as **Cracker** (1993-95, 1996, 2006), **The West Wing** (1999-2006) and **Buffy the Vampire Slayer** (1997-2003) had characters change and develop as a result of their adventures. Relationships formed and dissolved, characters matured in response to circumstance. These weren't the leads of 1960s and 70s shows such as John Steed, George Dixon or James T Kirk, essentially unchanged from first to last episodes. These dramas developed with their characters; you would find it hard to tell the same story in the same way from year to year. This had the benefit of keeping the drama fresh, quietly reformatting the show on an annual basis. Russell T Davies had developed his career in series

---

[35] For instance, during *The Greatest Show in the Galaxy* (1988) Ace acquires an earring which she then appropriates as a badge; however this badge is clearly visible in the preceding story *Silver Nemesis*.

such as **Springhill** (1996-97), **Revelations** (1994-96) and **The Grand** (1997-98), which had all depended on ongoing character development; equally his work leading up to **Doctor Who** had been series focussing on characters and relationships. The old conception of the Doctor was no longer an option; he would go from simply being the lead role in an action series to the lead character. Character flourishes would no longer be adequate; the lead role would require a capable actor.

With this in mind it's easy to see why Davies was horrified to see names such as Paul Daniels linked to the role[36]; it placed the series firmly back in a light entertainment tradition rather than a dramatic one. Daniels was a stage magician by trade; his name being mentioned in connection with the series affirmed that it was still not being taken seriously in some quarters. This perception was a challenge; at the time of being announced as **Doctor Who**'s head writer Davies had forged a reputation for provocative drama with the likes of **Queer as Folk** (1999-2000) and **The Second Coming** (2003), but Davies's name being attached still wasn't enough to shed patronising perceptions of a lightweight show. The series lacked an obvious element of gravitas, a statement of intent that would cause this perception to be revised.

It's fortunate then that Hugh Grant turned down the role[37]. He may have been unlikely ever to accept, but his reputation would not have been such a statement of intent. He had risen to fame with

---

[36] 'Paul Daniels to Be Doctor Who'.

[37] Davies, Russell T, 'Production Notes #3: Coffee and TV'. DWM #343. Grant had briefly played the Doctor in the 1999 Comic Relief sketch *The Curse of Fatal Death*.

lead roles in Richard Curtis movies such as *Four Weddings and a Funeral* (1994), *Notting Hill* (1999) and *Love Actually* (2003), perfecting an image as a very English light comedy bumbler. He would have had the star quality, but not necessarily a heavyweight acting reputation[38]. Instead the actor eventually chosen for the lead role would provide both name recognition and the necessary reputation: Christopher Eccleston.

Eccleston had risen to fame in acclaimed dramatic roles. After his breakthrough as Derek Bentley in *Let Him Have It* (1991) Eccleston had made his reputation as a DCI Bilborough in **Cracker** and as Nicky Hutchinson in the prestige drama **Our Friends in the North** (1996). Eccleston was not an actor who fitted the more aristocratic template of the previous Doctors, his best known roles all being characters from working-class backgrounds. The actors who had played the Doctor for the BBC in the 20th century were all well-spoken: Hartnell, Troughton, Jon Pertwee, Davison and Colin Baker all spoke with the well-modulated tones of southern England and Tom Baker's rich tones betrayed little hint of his Liverpool origins. Even Sylvester McCoy's Scottish accent sounds well-bred. Only with *Doctor Who* (1996) did a working-class accent creep in, and even then Paul McGann's costume and long-haired wig strongly signified that this was the same middle-class show about an alien aristocrat it had always been.

---

[38] A vision of what might have been can be glimpsed in *The Curse of Fatal Death* where Grant's as polite, bumbling and aristocratic as you'd expect.

Gareth Roberts described the 20th-century Doctors as having 'the air of lordly Edwardian philanthropists, stepping in from a position of privilege to help the little people'[39]. It's a vision rooted in the dying colonial days the show was conceived in: a beneficent representative of a more advanced culture bringing civilisation to the rest of the universe. It's one of the first tropes Davies identifies and dispenses with, purely in casting Eccleston. This Doctor would have nothing of the aristocracy about him; quite the opposite. His outfit is defiantly ordinary compared to previous Doctors; where their outfits deliberately marked them as apart from contemporary British cultural norms his is an attempt to blend in: leather jacket, v-neck jumper, black trousers and leather boots. There's no equivalent of Tom Baker's infamous scarf or the question-mark motif of the 1980s Doctors. Similarly his hairstyle is short, utilitarian[40]. And the episode makes a point of drawing attention to this Doctor's Mancunian accent: Rose notes that it would lead her to suspect him of being a domestic alien, a Northerner in southern England rather than a being from another planet. And, bringing him even closer to the level of humans, he becomes emotionally involved with a human being.

Rose, fundamentally, is the beginning of a love story; of a Time Lord and a human meeting, realising that they can bring something to the lives of the other that they lack. Rose lacks excitement,

---

[39] Roberts, Gareth, 'Guess Who?'. DWM Special Edition #11: *The Doctor Who Companion: Series One*.

[40] At the time of his casting McGann had his hair cut short (for the SAS drama *The One That Got Away* (1996)); however the **Doctor Who** production team had insisted on his wearing a wig.

adventure and the opportunity to realise her potential, the Doctor lacks an emotional connection to the wider universe. The Doctor having an emotional fondness for human beings has plenty of precedents: it can be seen with his companions and particularly in his sadness at their departure – the Doctor's soliloquy in *The Massacre* (1966) and his low-key departure from Jo's engagement celebrations in *The Green Death* (1973) being the two best examples – but it's rarely had a romantic frisson before[41]. This is the key reinvention Russell T Davies brought to the Doctor's character; to reinvent him as a romantic hero for an ongoing series, building on the direction hinted at in the 1996 TV movie.

Prior to 1996 the character of the Doctor had to be seen to be above romance; the nature of the series, which dictated an older male actor accompanied mainly by young females, might have unfortunate connotations. Indeed this is how Susan came to be the Doctor's granddaughter; after the cast structure was decided, it was considered that the Doctor could not be seen simply to be travelling the universe with a random teenager, hence the familial connection to avoid awkward questions[42]. This rule held through the 1980s with John Nathan-Turner's diktat of 'no hanky panky in

---

[41] There is a certain romantic element suggested in his relationship with fellow Time Lord Romana during the show's 17th season, but this is suggested more in performance than script, and is down to the real-life romantic relationship between Tom Baker and Lalla Ward at the time.
[42] Howe, David J, Stammers, Mark, Walker, Stephen James, *Doctor Who The Handbook – The First Doctor*, p200.

the TARDIS'[43] explicitly excluding any hint of romantic entanglement between the Doctor and his companions. The few exceptions saw this lack of sexual interest played for comedy, such as the Doctor misunderstanding Cameca's offer of sharing cocoa in *The Aztecs* (1964).

Only in the 1990s did this change, primarily with the advent of Paul McGann's younger, passionate Doctor. He became the first Doctor to kiss a companion, and whilst the first kiss may have been simply an act of pure joy, the second kiss, at the climax to the episode, is certainly a more romantic act. This aspect was picked up on in the nascent slash fiction scene and in the original novels based on the series during the 1990s and early 2000s – the climax to Virgin Publishing's final **Doctor Who New Adventures** novel, *The Dying Days* (1997), features a scene heavily hinting at companion Bernice Summerfield initiating sex with the Doctor, and the BBC Books novel *The Year of Intelligent Tigers* (2001) is centred around a relationship between the Doctor and a male musician, Karl. The TV movie's great contribution to **Doctor Who** was to enable a smoother transition between the plot-driven action series model the show had followed since the Hartnell era and Davies's version, which prioritised character. *Rose* renders *Doctor Who* (1996) a stepping-stone rather than an anachronism; there is no longer any real taboo for Davies to break by putting the Doctor-companion relationship at the heart of the episode.

---

[43] For an example, see Grieves, Robert T, 'Video: Who's Who in Outer Space'. The line was notorious enough to be referenced in *Kill the Moon* (2014).

The decision to present the opening story of the 2005 season from Rose's viewpoint means the element of attraction is presented as natural to the audience; the Doctor may be explicitly alien but he appears human and there's no hint of his age as yet. For the purposes of placing the Doctor and Rose's relationship at the heart of the show we're encouraged instead to go with the superficial impression that he's simply a slightly older man[44]. The general audience does not have the information that the Doctor is centuries old as yet, nor are they remotely encouraged to consider whether the Doctor's alien biology and Rose's human biology might be compatible[45]. It's presented as a perfectly natural thing within the fiction; the Doctor and Rose are as defined by their relationship as are the lead characters in other series Davies has created; Vince and Stuart in **Queer as Folk**, the eponymous characters in **Bob & Rose** (2001) and Stephen and Judith in **The Second Coming**[46].

---

[44] This element is dealt with in the first few minutes of *Aliens of London* where Jackie naturally assumes her daughter disappearing for a year with an older man implies an unhealthy relationship. In the wake of Operation Yewtree it's interesting to speculate whether a show designed for primetime on a Saturday evening would have been safe making such a joke.

[45] This avoidance of an awkward question is an uncommon occurrence in fiction, with egregious examples such as Superman and Lois Lane also largely turning a blind eye to the complications of interspecies relationships. However, SF author Larry Niven did consider the prospect of Kryptonian-human intercourse in his 1969 essay 'Man of Steel, Woman of Kleenex'.

[46] This remains consistent in his later writing, with **Cucumber** (2015) being centred around the relationship between Henry and Lance.

What's notable about these other Davies-created series is that they comprise limited runs, one or two series at most. The nature of writing about relationships in depth as Davies favours means that there is generally a limited scope for a series to explore – after a period the course of the relationship will be played out and the characters changed from what made them an attractive pairing to follow in the first place[47].

Rose presents the Doctor as someone you couldn't help but be attracted to: his first act in the revived series is to save Rose's life, an act which naturally leaves a good impression. He's presented as being in control of an unfamiliar situation throughout, despite the pace of their initial meeting being frenetic (according to the notes on time of day in the script, the time for Rose between descending to the basement with the lottery money and exiting after the Doctor's warning to run for her life is five minutes[48]). Although he does not proffer explanations at this point, he clearly knows the reasons for the shop window dummies coming to life and a method

---

[47] Davies's version of **Doctor Who** overcame this limitation by changing the regular cast every season and therefore presenting a different mix of elements; whilst this was down to circumstance, the pace of change in terms of onscreen characters is notable. Christopher Eccleston departs after one season, Billie Piper after the second year, Freema Agyeman lasts one year as Martha, Catherine Tate stays one season as Donna and the final set of specials had no fixed companion. This contrasts with Steven Moffat's version of the show, which has seen the companions remain in place for several seasons.

[48] She enters the basement at '1803' and exits at '1808' according to the script as presented in Davies, *The Shooting Scripts* pp 13, 17.

to defeat them[49]. This ends with him blowing up Rose's place of work. It's clear that he offers a life of excitement and cares about humans enough to save her life.

This is immediately contrasted to her boyfriend Mickey. Although the script describes him as 'cheeky, laddish, a good catch'[50], he prioritises his own pleasure in watching football in the pub over looking after Rose after she's witnessed her place of work exploding. When she asks to use his computer to investigate the Doctor he tells her not to read his emails, indicating he has something to hide. Mickey is essentially selfish in the partnership – for all that he's dubbed a 'good catch' he offers Rose nothing more than a mundane relationship; one where there is a lack of trust on his part. This contrast will deepen further during the episode; faced with the Autons and Nestene Consciousness later on he's terrified 'like an animal' and, although it's played down in the episode, Rose's line 'oh you're stinking' indicates he's soiled himself[51]. Mickey is incapable of dealing with an unfamiliar situation; along with the job and council flat he represents elements holding Rose back that are 'make do' rather than fulfilling; the Doctor represents excitement, escape and the possibility of realising her potential.

Any hint of a sexual element is dampened by their second meeting. Although Rose invites the Doctor in, after he's clearly piqued her curiosity, he turns down Jackie's attempted seduction, prioritising a mystery signal related to the Nestene invasion that he's detected in

---

[49] The Doctor does not explain, but dismisses Rose's fairly logical explanations.
[50] Davies, *The Shooting Scripts* p12.
[51] Davies, *The Shooting Scripts* pp38-39.

the flat. He's quite happy to engage when the flirting is mild but ends the conversation quickly when Jackie shows an interest in taking things further. The following scene in the flat sums up Davies's vision for the Doctor; for all that he has knowledge and abilities beyond those of humans he's still a fallible being – he apparently reads a whole paperback in a second, and disables the Auton arm Rose has brought back to the flat, but cannot pull off the attempted curved shuffle of cards. As will also later happen with David Tennant's interpretation, this Doctor's great power is worn lightly, particularly with people he's not familiar with. Rose's attempt to get him to talk about the dummies coming to life can be seen as paralleling the way Jackie's advances were rejected; Rose rationalises things with a light-hearted enquiry as to whether the living dummies are an attempt to take over Britain's shops, but the Doctor stops this line of inquiry by pointing out that the creatures she met 'want to overthrow the human race. And destroy you.'[52]

At this point Rose is incapable of comprehending the Doctor's world, a point he underlines with his speech about the 'turn of the Earth'[53]. The Doctor has the requisite nature of the romantic hero, enigmatic and apparently beyond Rose's reach. It's an impression only reinforced by her conversation with Clive – Clive builds the Doctor up as an ominous immortal presence whose appearance presages death and destruction. To some extent she's beneath his notice when the fate of humanity is at stake, simply another human caught up in his affairs.

---

[52] Davies, *The Shooting Scripts* p24.
[53] Davies, *The Shooting Scripts* p25.

The key scenes between the two occur during and immediately after Rose's first trip in the TARDIS, where the dynamics of what will become their relationship are presented. This gives us the outline of the great flaw of the Doctor and the reason he chooses to make her the offer of travelling with him. While he's almost monomaniacally obsessed with stopping the Nestene scheme, he shows no indication of the human cost. After he has obtained the head of Mickey's Auton duplicate to allow him to track the controlling signal to the Nestene lair, Rose asks him the question any concerned human would in the circumstances: she asks him if Mickey has been killed. Tellingly the Doctor's response is that he 'didn't think of that'[54]. He thinks on a grander scale, not even considering the individual toll. It's almost as if he's lost the ability to consider individual lives, but this is not something expanded upon in this episode[55]. From *Rose* alone it would simply be indicative of his alien nature.

This, however, is a flaw in his character which Rose can correct; she can be his conscience as Jiminy Cricket is to Pinocchio. She reminds him of the human consequences of his actions – he has already

---

[54] Davies, *The Shooting Scripts* p34.

[55] This is retrospectively explained in *The Day of the Doctor* (2013) as the War Doctor using the Moment to end the Time War by wiping out both Time Lords and Daleks – the ninth Doctor's inability to consider individual lives is therefore apparently a consequence of the genocidal decision he made; a safeguard for his sanity. In this light, the change in causality which undoes the decision without changing this Doctor's memories is almost unimaginably cruel to this incarnation, and renders him a kind of sacrifice to the Doctor's conscience.

ignored her attempted conversation in the flat about the dead electrician Wilson, to track down the signal being given off by the Auton arm; here he continues his obsession with tracking down the control signal. In this conversation he fails to consider an individual victim of the Autons not once, but twice. Rose has run through the consequences in her mind – of having to tell his mother – and calls the Doctor out twice on his failure to consider Mickey's potential death. The Doctor's response is indicative of his grand-scale thinking: '...I'm busy trying to save the life of every stupid ape blundering about on top of this planet...'[56] This is where they realise each other's true natures, and where the romance that will play out over two seasons begins. From the Doctor's point of view, Rose reminds him of the consequences his actions may have and is unafraid to call him out if she believes he is wrong. The rest of the scene is played more lightly, with a tone of almost friendly banter. A relationship has clearly been established; symbolically, their run across Westminster Bridge is undertaken hand in hand. The Doctor is clearly aware of Rose's worth by this point, and her subsequent actions to save his life in the Nestene lair only reinforce that decision.

What we also learn from the Doctor's confrontation and conversation with the Nestene Consciousness is what drives him: that for all the superior façade he's presented to Rose during the episode he's driven by an awareness of his own inadequacies and often rendered powerless by them. He is driven by survivor's guilt, a topical motivation in 2005, seen in veterans of the initial Gulf War

---

[56] Davies, *The Shooting Scripts* p35.

and the 2003 invasion of Iraq. He clearly recognises that the Consciousness has a point when it accuses him of a war crime (unspecified because of its lack of actual dialogue). He's wracked by the guilt of being unable to save not only the Nestene's world but an unspecified number of others. In the moment where decisive action is needed it renders him powerless, held captive by an Auton while the final phase of the invasion commences, and reduced to urging Rose to get away.

This introduces a recurrent theme of the season – this Doctor rarely takes the decisive action required to resolve a story, but instead inspires others to do so. Rose's willingness to use her limited gymnastic skills saves the day here; Charles Dickens takes the decisive action in *The Unquiet Dead*; Mickey in *World War Three*; the Dalek's suicide is the key action in *Dalek*; Cathica brings down the Jagrafess in *The Long Game*; Pete's self-sacrifice heals the wound in time in *Father's Day*; Jack is willing to lay down his life to stop a bomb falling in *The Doctor Dances*; and Blon is persuaded to look into the heart of the TARDIS in *Boom Town* (all 2005). Each is inspired to take action after a conversation with the Doctor, but each takes action where the Doctor physically or morally cannot. This unwillingness to take a decisive action is a clear and deliberate theme which plays out across the season, and is key to *The Parting of the Ways* and the resolution of the eventual Bad Wolf arc plot[57]. It may also explain this incarnation of the Doctor trying to force humour at crucial times; if he's been traumatised by the events of

---

[57] This is perfectly in line with the action we see taken in *The Day of the Doctor*; having made such a decision once, his unwillingness to face such consequences again is entirely logical.

the war, a perversely jovial tone might help avoid situations becoming bad enough for him to have to make some kind of decision[58].

The object of the episode then is to render the Doctor a fascinating character once again; in brutal terms the aim is to have the audience replicate Rose's climactic decision to travel with him. What we learn about the character is in Eccleston's performance and the sparse hints dropped into the script – an absolute minimum. We know he's an alien with superior knowledge and technology; we know he can travel in time and space and he fought in a war. There's no other backstory required nor stated, the hook for the audience is entirely in the character they've just met. The Autons, despite having met the Doctor twice before onscreen, are never named, nor does the Doctor ever mention those previous encounters to Rose. This Doctor avoids discussing his past where possible; Rose learns more concrete information about the Doctor's past from Clive than she does from the Doctor himself. He explains himself to her with the 'turn of the Earth', speech but doesn't address his past with her directly until *The End of the World*, at a point when he feels comfortable doing so. *Rose* simply asks us to accept the character as he is now, at face value. For the first time in the show's history we're being asked to follow the Doctor because of who he is, not because of what he does.

---

[58] Although Eccleston indicated whilst promoting the series **Safe House** (2015) that he believes he misplayed the comedy and would perform this very differently now, the inability to quite get a joke right is perfectly in character.

Rose finally puts the Doctor himself at the heart of the story which bears his name. Amidst the flashier, more obvious reformatting of the series, the episode finally turns the Doctor into a dramatic character in his own right; one who is affected by the consequences of his own decisions instead of simply moving on to the next story – and with this change it will become difficult for the series to shift episodes about during a season as it used to do[59]. Through our viewpoint character, Rose, we're shown how fascinating, frustrating and fantastic he can be. This version of the Doctor is Russell T Davies making his childhood hero a viable lead character in a 21st century drama series: a mythic character reformatted for a new generation. An old hero made new.

---

[59] This is ably demonstrated when *The Curse of the Black Spot* and *Night Terrors* had their broadcast order swapped; with the events of *A Good Man Goes To War* (all 2011), which see Amy's child kidnapped, a conversation between Rory and Amy making light of missing children and their fears looks particularly callous.

CHAPTER 3: 'NICE TO MEET YOU, ROSE'

'2 INT. ROSE'S BEDROOM DAY 1 0730

'CU a black, square alarm clock. A hand slams it off. ROSE TYLER sits up in bed, gathers herself for a second. She's 19, her bedroom's a mess, she's got another bloody day at work, and she's so much better than this. Ho hum.'

['Rose', *Doctor Who: The Shooting Scripts*][60]

Doctor Who in 2005 begins as it did in 1963; following the exploits of ordinary Londoners who become mixed up in the Doctor's adventures. 'An Unearthly Child' sees the teachers Ian Chesterton and Barbara Wright investigate a strange pupil in their school who in many ways has incredibly advanced knowledge while on other, more ordinary matters, is naïve. We first encounter the Doctor as a result of their investigation; the story we enter is not the Doctor's, it's theirs. With over 50 years having passed since, it's easy to forget that the Doctor was not initially the star of his own show. The character's name gives the show its title, and William Hartnell is always the first actor credited, but the underlying story that propels the series until *The Chase* (1965) is Ian and Barbara's quest to return to their own time. They act to ground the strange world of the Doctor and provide a contemporary viewpoint on the events we see in Earth history or on alien worlds. Whatever the Doctor encounters – Aztecs, Sensorites, Daleks, a planet where giant ants battle giant butterflies – they serve to keep the viewer from becoming too alienated.

---

[60] Davies, *The Shooting Scripts* p12.

This makes them outliers in terms of **Doctor Who** companions. Of the companions during the remainder of 20th-century **Doctor Who**, only Steven truly carries a whole story by himself (*The Massacre*). With Innes Lloyd and Gerry Davis reformatting the series from one about exploration to a more standard 1960s adventure format, the companions become mainly a plot function, asking questions and keeping the plot moving. Verity Lambert's era is rightly celebrated for establishing **Doctor Who**, but the changes made by Lloyd and Davis have greater consequences. They move the Doctor to centre stage, allowing him to initiate adventures and become the central character, something that's made more overt by the introduction of Patrick Troughton as the Doctor. He is better able to carry the role of action-series lead than the older Hartnell. But this also makes the role of the companion far less interesting, and for all the quirks and foibles of various characters their roles are essentially interchangeable. And to maintain their ability to keep the plot moving they're in stasis character-wise – Jamie and Zoe are left unchanged by their travels thanks to memory wipes, Liz Shaw returns to Cambridge, Sarah Jane apparently returns to journalism.[61] Even Leela, expressly written to be developed from an alien savage to something more civilised, is all but indistinguishable in character from first story to last, before she suddenly decides she fancies a random Time Lord. The only character development

---

[61] The 2006 episode *School Reunion* imposes a degree of retrospective character development on Sarah Jane to explore its theme of the effect the Doctor has on the lives of the people he travels with, but mainly limits this to a backstory of the time after she left the Doctor. It also ignores the events of *The Five Doctors* (1983) to present its theme more elegantly.

we tend to see comes in the stories where companions have to be written out. Jo leaves to marry a man she sees as a human version of the Doctor; Romana's sole development before suddenly being inspired to become an interuniversal refugee coordinator is when she regenerates due to Mary Tamm's departure; and Tegan is just as suddenly sickened by the violence of the Doctor's adventures[62].

It's only with Ace's introduction that a nod is made in the direction of consistent character development. Ace has a convoluted, unlikely background – a bolshie London teenager with a fascination for explosives, who finds herself waiting tables on another world after being caught in a time storm. Character development isn't particularly evident in season 25 – even her betrayal by potential boyfriend Mike in *Remembrance of the Daleks* (1988) is never mentioned again – but kicks in during season 26. In the last three stories of the 1989 season we see Ace coming to terms with past traumas: an act of arson (*Ghost Light*), confronting her relationship with her mother (*The Curse of Fenric*), and dealing with the onset of adulthood and the complications it brings (*Survival*). It's a brave attempt to move the show onwards, but these don't build on each other, partly due to the switches of story order between production and broadcast, and partly due to the show being removed from the air. However, they were originally designed as part of a character arc to show the Doctor training Ace up for his

---

[62] At the end of *Resurrection of the Daleks*, which has the highest onscreen body count in series history. Why this is more traumatic than the Master killing her aunt then wiping out half the universe, possession by the Mara, the death of Adric or the slaughter on Sea Base Four is never satisfactorily explained.

own purposes, forcing her to grow from the teenage waitress of *Dragonfire* (1987) to an independent woman worthy of attending the Time Lord Academy[63]. Production circumstances ultimately mean the character development is flawed, but there is a clear intent to test the limits of the traditional companion role, beyond asking questions to progress the plot and providing someone to rescue. Arguably these last three stories of Season 26 are the first time the show has consistently been about the companions since the Hartnell era.

Retaining this old model of companion would be an anachronism for a major drama series in 2005. With the Doctor reformatted from the lead in an adventure series to a character in his own right, capable of changing and developing, it was also necessary to redefine the role of the companion. This lack of development is a function of the nature of **Doctor Who**'s adventure series format, the ongoing series of adventures needing the Doctor and companion to fulfil archetypal roles for the stories to function. At some points this is clearly an absurdity to viewers weaned on more character-led TV, most egregiously in *Time-Flight* episode 1, where Adric's traumatic death in *Earthshock* is dealt with in one short scene and then forgotten. For most of its 20th-century run the series simply isn't interested in character or consequence – it's a plot-driven anthology series linked by different events happening

---

[63] The intended conclusion to Ace's story was later made as *Thin Ice* (2011), part of Big Finish Productions' **Lost Stories** range of audio dramas, although Ace's ultimate destiny was amended. Alternative developments for the character were also presented in Virgin's **New Adventures** range and the *Doctor Who Magazine* comic strip.

to the same people. For all its adaptability of format, **Doctor Who** was left behind by the wider televisual context, the refinements made by Innes Lloyd and Gerry Davis in 1966 to turn the series into a more straightforward plot-driven adventure show still being essentially unchanged in 1989.

Russell T Davies's reformatting of the series from action-adventure to action-drama meant that the role of the companion would have to change profoundly. With the new series essentially operating as a drama based around the relationship of the two leads, the new companion would have to not only answer the question of why they would travel with the Doctor but why the Doctor would choose them. As far back as 1999 he'd opined that the series would have to be '...more personal, more emotional' in response to what he perceived as'...the whole of television... becoming a bit more character-led'. He pointed out the 'shallow character development' and even dismissed the developments with Ace as 'slight, ephemeral notions of characterisation'[64]. It's a clear critique that even then he saw the show's format and the role of the companion in particular as requiring updating; that his version of the show would make his companions stronger, more rounded characters.

It was clear from the casting that the new companion would be more integral to the series than simply asking questions and passing test tubes; for all the dramatic credibility Christopher Eccleston brought to the role of the Doctor, Billie Piper brought in a younger audience familiar with her from her successful pop career

---

[64] 'We're Gonna Be Bigger Than Star Wars!'.

and newspaper gossip columns.[65]. Davies had entertained the notion of being 'a bit cynical and commercial'[66] in the casting of a companion as far back as that 1999 interview, and this recognition factor was clearly part of the thinking behind Piper's recruitment five years later. Of the actors previously cast in companion roles, the only ones with similar levels of prior fame were William Russell (who had starred in **The Adventures of Sir Lancelot** (1956-57)) and Bonnie Langford (famed for her role as Violet Elizabeth Bott in the 1977 version of **Just William** and light entertainment such as **The Hot Shoe Show** (1983-84) and the musical *Cats*)[67]. Piper would bring an ideal mixture of publicity and acting ability to the role; looking back with 10 years of hindsight it's hard to imagine that there could have been any other choice. Although in acting terms Piper was a rising star, casting such a prominent name was a statement of the importance of the companion's role in the new

---

[65] At this time Piper was in a relationship with the DJ Chris Evans, which was seen as somewhat scandalous due to their 16-year age difference.

[66] 'We're Gonna Be Bigger Than Star Wars!'.

[67] Langford, Piper's most direct precedent, was an unhelpful comparison; she was perceived as a light entertainer rather than a dramatic actor, and the troubled nature of **Doctor Who**'s production during her time on the show meant she was seen as part of the show's problems. It was also an unfair comparison; Piper's pop career was a diversion from an intended acting career which came about when she was spotted by producers in an advert for *Smash Hits* magazine. She had several roles behind her before playing Rose, including high-profile roles in a modern retelling of Chaucer's *The Miller's Tale* (2003) and the title role in *Bella and the Boys* (2004).

series, as was the companion's name appearing in the opening credits alongside that of the actor playing the Doctor.

The other anachronism that the new series had to correct was the deliberately masculine viewpoint the series had taken. The default model of the series is to have stories centre round the Doctor, an alien who always manifested as male[68]. While certain characters had been conceived as equals, or able to challenge the Doctor (Romana as a Time Lady of superior ability, Sarah Jane as a feminist, Tegan being prepared to argue back), the series largely revolved around the lead character. This means that, with a few exceptions such as *The Aztecs* or *Survival*, the stories have always been presented from a male point of view. The series therefore naturally skewed towards a male audience, with the female leads largely reacting and largely subservient to the male lead. This is something Russell T Davies made a point of correcting:

> 'You cannot have subsidiary female characters. I knew exactly what I was after: women viewers. They're very specifically targeted by this series, because I know that they don't automatically watch science fiction. It's considered to be a man's thing, so I was absolutely, specifically, after women. Why cut out half the population?'[69]

---

[68] It is later confirmed in the episodes *The Doctor's Wife* (2011) and *Dark Water* (2014) that gender is fluid for Gallifreyans.

[69] Russell T Davies, DWM #359, quoted in DWM Special Edition #24: *In Their Own Words Volume 6: 1997-2009*, p23. Davies does not stop at emphasising Rose as a strong character in her own right but actively looks to reverse gender roles: Mickey is the one who gets

The character of Rose would be an instant correction to this. The series is still called **Doctor Who**, but the description initially assigned to this first episode ('Rose meets the Doctor, and the journey begins', later shortened to *Rose Meets The Doctor*[70], finally to simply *Rose*) emphasised the importance of the companion to the series. It is also visible in the trailers for the show – along with the trailers with Christopher Eccleston promising 'the trip of a lifetime', there is one concentrating on Rose and the decision she'll have to make in the first episode between her normal life and travelling with the Doctor. Further to this, *Rose*, and indeed the rest of the season, is narrated largely from her point of view. Partly this is to emphasise the human viewpoint of the Doctor's world for viewers, but it's equally a statement that this version of **Doctor Who** will embrace a female viewpoint: the female lead (and therefore the female perspective) is now as important as the male lead, perhaps even more so[71]. The world we're initially invited into is hers, the concerns we're initially invited to share are hers. The frenetic opening montage establishes her life and world; where she lives, her living arrangements, her boyfriend and her job. This could

---

himself captured and is helpless until rescued, and when Mickey's Auton duplicate has his head pulled off in the restaurant it is a man who screams.

[70] Russell T Davies, 'Pitch Perfect'. DWM Special Edition, *The Doctor Who Companion Series One* p43.

[71] This has arguably only been the case twice before: most clearly with Barbara Wright who, like Rose, acts as the Doctor's moral conscience. A case may be also be made for the second Romana, who often acts as a more competent version of the Doctor in the 17th season. In the latter case, however, the Doctor still dominates the adventures.

be an establishing scene from almost any modern drama series – it's pacey, with plenty of fast cuts underscored by a soundtrack with the energy of modern pop music[72].

In the first few seconds of the new series the emphasis has already shifted from plot to character, to the extent we learn more about Rose in 90 seconds than we do about any previous companion in their entire time in the show. We know her relationship, her family set-up, where's she's from, her job and her social status within minutes of her introduction. Compared to previous companions, who've usually had full stories to introduce themselves, this is speed-dating. Davies holds off on introducing any science fiction elements until he's welcomed the audience into a familiar world that could pass for our own and established Rose herself as on avatar of normality. It's a world of council estates, unsatisfying relationships and dead-end jobs.

Rose could simply continue on in this limited world for the rest of her life, perhaps unaware of there being anything greater in the universe. It's one of the minor tragedies of human existence, that so much potential goes untapped and unfulfilled simply because of opportunities to shine being denied by circumstance, or ignorance of those opportunities. Davies' work has a fascination with ordinary mortals picked out for a great destiny by random fate – Steven Baxter, a video shop worker, becoming the Son of God in **The Second Coming** (2003), Max Vivaldi discovering he owns the city of

---

[72] The initial guide track for this opening montage, before Murray Gold's score was added, was 'Sound of the Underground' by Girls Aloud.

Swansea in **Mine All Mine** (2004) or Donna Noble, the ordinary typist seemingly being destined by prophecy to be extraordinary, in Davies' fourth **Doctor Who** series (2008). Davies believes in the power of the ordinary person, as opposed to inherent natural superiority to other people. The point of these characters is their very ordinariness: the fact that, as the National Lottery promised when it began, 'It could be you'.

This is the key to Rose's success, beyond even Billie Piper's performance. She isn't the dreaded cliché of a 'strong woman'; she is an ordinary, flawed and all too human woman. What marks her out as being fit to travel with the Doctor isn't an inherently superior ability to other people, it's her moral sense, her willingness to hold the Doctor to account and, in a situation with the fate of the world at stake, to use the limited resources she has to attempt to resolve the situation. Until she meets the Doctor she's happy to settle for a comfortable relationship rather than an exciting one; a job which helps her get by rather than fulfils her – this is visible in that first montage where she's reactive instead of proactive; to the alarm clock, to Mickey and to the hand that waves the envelope containing lottery money in front of her just as she's about to leave. She does what's expected of her. Her chance encounter with the Doctor is the catalyst for her overcoming these flaws and realising her potential. Further character flaws will manifest themselves more clearly across the course of the 2005 season (particularly in *Father's Day* and in her treatment of Mickey in *Boom Town*), but simultaneously the potential we see being realised will also be demonstrated (showing compassion to a Dalek in *Dalek* and saving the day in both the current episode and *The Parting of the Ways*).

It is this active choice which also marks her out as different from previous companions. For most there was some coercive factor which led them to travel with the Doctor: Ian and Barbara were kidnapped, Steven and Vicki stranded a long way from home without any hope of rescue, and others had lost family members (Victoria, Leela, Nyssa, Tegan and Peri all fall into this category). And even once that decision is taken the Doctor is unable to control the destination of his TARDIS and thereby unable to return them to their own time[73]. Once they decide to travel with the Doctor (or the decision is made for them) there is rarely any reconsideration of that decision until their exit story; only with Tegan's departure in *Time-Flight* and re-joining in *Arc of Infinity* (1983) does the motivation for travelling with the Doctor change.

Rose's life, as outlined in that opening montage, is one of quiet content, if not fulfilment. There is no real pressing need for her to go with the Doctor; although her job is gone with Henrik's destroyed, she has her life with her home, family and boyfriend to consider. The Doctor must persuade her that he's worth travelling with; although Rose pursues him following their meeting at the flat, attempting to track him down by visiting Clive, the situation has reversed by the end of the episode. Initially it appears that even the excitement of foiling the Auton invasion has not been enough to overcome her sense of duty. The promise of travelling anywhere

---

[73] This is retconned in *The Doctor's Wife* with Idris, personifying the TARDIS, telling the Doctor she always took him where he needed to go. Perhaps this explanation for the Doctor's inconsistent control of his vehicle is a retrospective indication as to which of the Doctor's companions the TARDIS thought were suitable to accompany him.

in the universe is not enough to overcome that sense of responsibility – she is concerned about her mum and what might become of Mickey if she leaves him. It's only with the promise of time travel, the Doctor returning like a shy boy on the edge of the dancefloor coyly offering one more thing that might overcome an initial knockback, that she changes her mind.

The whole episode is about this choice; the monsters and explosions are simply there to get Rose to meet the Doctor and make her decision. There are no coercive elements to this choice; for the first time the companion has a degree of their own agency, a comfortable life they can return to. Rose proves with her actions in the Nestene lair that she's someone the Doctor considers worthy of travelling with him, but equally the Doctor must prove worthy of Rose accepting his offer. The decision which catalyses the series is one made in equal part by the Doctor and Rose. It is clear that, no matter that this is a relationship between a time-travelling alien and a working-class shop assistant, it's a relationship of equals. The Doctor must choose to offer an adventure in time and space to Rose for there to be an adventure in the first place; Rose must make the choice to accompany the Doctor for herself and for the audience. Rose is therefore the key role in this story and the revival; if her joy at the opportunity to accompany the Doctor were not sold by acting and direction then the purpose of the episode would remain unachieved. In that sense, she **is** the audience, their way into the Doctor's world.

This use of the companion as the viewer's 'eyes and ears'[74] is also a return to the early days of the show. Over the course of the 20th century run, the function of the companion had moved away from being an identification figure for the viewer. Susan was envisaged by Sydney Newman as helping young boys and girls with audience identification[75] and Ian and Barbara provided the audience's eyes and ears. This, however, changed as the show progressed – Dodo, Ben and Polly and the companions of the UNIT era (including Sarah Jane) are the only companions from contemporary Earth between 1966 and 1986. The remaining companions are alien in terms of location, whether this is temporal (ranging from 18th-century Scotsmen to space pilots and savages from the far future, geographic (Australian or American) or that of being a different species[76]. Even Ace, ostensibly a contemporary character modelled on teenagers Ian Briggs had tutored at Questors Youth Theatre[77], came with a convoluted backstory which meant she could never truly act as a viewpoint character.

Since 2005, however, **Doctor Who** has always maintained a companion with a contemporary viewpoint; Rose, Mickey, Martha,

[74] Tribe, Steve, *Doctor Who: Companions and Allies*, p62.
[75] Howe, David J, Mark Stammers and Stephen James Walker, *Doctor Who: The Sixties*, p4.
[76] This includes Time Lords, Trions and robots; Adric is even from a different universe entirely.
[77] Sullivan, Shannon Patrick, 'Dragonfire', *A Brief History of Time (Travel)*.

Donna, Amy, Rory and Clara[78] have all been drawn from contemporary settings, and even when there is a futuristic companion such as Jack, we still have a character the audience can identify with to ground the show. In practice this limits the lifespan of a companion; after a series of adventures with the Doctor, the character will be so changed by their experiences that the audience will be less able to relate to them. The weight of their experiences will change them so much that any conceit that they represent the audience will become unconvincing. By the end of her first season, Rose has run off with an alien, seen the Earth die, saved her father only to see him die again, and ascended to godhood[79]. This is a fundamental conflict at the heart of the way Davies uses the science fiction elements **Doctor Who** to propel his drama; the story he wishes to tell is of the romance between the Doctor and Rose, whereas the experiences she has are so extraordinary their cumulative psychological impact would mean she became somewhat alien to the audience. Davies undercuts this with his companions by concentrating on the emotion of the drama; he is interested in the science fiction trappings of the series only inasmuch as they allow him to tell the story he wants to tell about

---

[78] Although Clara's introduction is convoluted with the 'Impossible Girl' storyline, the version of her who joins the Doctor in *The Bells of Saint John* (2013) is entirely contemporary.

[79] However, she has not yet visited an alien world onscreen, although dialogue in *Boom Town* indicates she's visited at least three: Justicia (a reference to the tie-in novel *The Monsters Inside*), San Kaloon and Woman Wept.

the romance between the Doctor and Rose[80]. Emotional logic, how people might plausibly react, will trump the mechanics of plot logic every time.

The success of Davies's **Doctor Who** is in a large degree down to this; that the reactions of his characters to ordinary events are naturalistic. It renders the world of the Doctor less alien, less strange[81] and therefore more enticing for a mass audience. It's therefore perhaps fortunate that Paul Abbott's proposed script for **Doctor Who**'s first season eventually fell through. It was to have revealed that Rose was the result of an experiment by the Doctor

---

[80] This explains a lot of fan complaints about the repeated use of 'deus ex machina' plot devices (a term not entirely accurately used by fans). In pure plot terms the resolutions of stories such as *The Parting of the Ways* (with Rose as the Bad Wolf intervening to save humanity from the Daleks), *Last of the Time Lords* (2007) (with the timeline of the Master's rule over Earth being erased) or *Journey's End* (Donna becoming a human-Time Lord hybrid and saving the day) may seem cheap, abrupt resolutions. However, in dramatic terms they make perfect sense, with the apotheoses of Rose and Donna being perhaps the ultimate expression of their empowerment by the Doctor, and the Master's rule ultimately being brought down by the faith in the Doctor engendered by Martha roaming the Earth for a year telling stories of him. The plot is less important than the impact on characters; with the changed nature of the series it's become a device to explore character.

[81] This contrasts with 'An Unearthly Child', where the oddness of the scenario of a time-travelling police box in a junkyard that's bigger on the inside than the outside is played up. In *Rose* the oddness of the TARDIS and an invasion by dummies is defrayed by being treated with humour.

to psychically breed the perfect companion[82], a revelation that would have undercut the purpose and point of Rose herself as established in the first episode. This would have negated Rose's virtue; her being an ordinary person who would act as the Doctor's conscience. The hard work of her introductory episode would be undermined by such a story, and it would have driven the Doctor's character to a manipulative extreme more typical of the seventh Doctor as envisaged by Andrew Cartmel, in the 1988 and 1989 seasons of the show and during the **New Adventures** era[83]. This would veer close to bringing eugenics and the ethics of such actions into the series: dark territory for a show being broadcast during Saturday teatimes. It's also difficult to see how it would have fitted into Rose's character arc for the first season, given that it renders her character subservient to the Doctor, vulnerable to his manipulation. It's strange to say that the both the 2005 series and the show as a whole are stronger for the absence of a writer of Abbott's calibre, but ultimately this was the correct creative decision.

In a wider sense *Rose* also acts as a direct template for the introduction of recurring companions. Both *Smith and Jones* (2007) and *Partners in Crime* (2008), which respectively introduce Martha and Donna as regular companions, are from the same model as

---

[82] Morley, Christopher, 'Doctor Who: Stories From The Scrapheap – The New Team/Pompeii'.

[83] The purest illustration of the intended manipulative nature of the seventh Doctor, and its foreseen and unforeseen consequences, can be found in Cartmel's War trilogy of books, *Cat's Cradle: Warhead*, *Warlock* and *Warchild*.

Rose. They repeat the storytelling trick of presenting the Doctor from the prospective companion's perspective, with the alien invasion storyline effectively a B-plot. The Doctor is introduced suddenly and surprisingly to Martha (in a piece of temporal sleight-of-hand that would later be seen as a hallmark of Steven Moffat's writing). She proves herself resourceful and worthy enough in ensuring the fugitive Plasmavore is caught by the Judoon, then reviving the Doctor so that the kidnapped hospital may be returned to Earth. We also meet her dysfunctional family; her parents are divorced and both brother and sister are uninterested in resolving family issues[84]. Finally she accepts an invitation from the Doctor, who returns to make her the offer of travelling with him. Donna's introduction is a touch more complicated, thanks to her prior appearance in *The Runaway Bride* (2006); she has met the Doctor and originally made the opposite choice to Rose: despite the Doctor showing her a more exciting life and clearly needing someone to act as a conscience, she initially chose to return to her more mundane existence. *Partners in Crime* sees her changing her mind and actively seeking the Doctor; whilst she has already

---

[84] The absence of a father figure in the companion's upbringing is clearly to the 21st century series what orphanhood was to the 20th century one; this lack of a father is possibly a further need the Doctor may fill in the lives of Rose and Martha. It's notable that the initial departures of both Rose and Martha coincide with their parents' relationships being restored; and that their final departures (and Donna's) involve them finding secure relationships of their own.

proven worthy of the Doctor by her actions in the previous story[85], she seeks him out much as Rose does and plays a key role in resolving the Adipose scheme. This can even be said to extend to Wilf in *The End of Time* (2009-10), who actively hunts down the Doctor and acts as his conscience. Even *The Eleventh Hour* (2010), which, similarly to *Rose*, has to introduce a new Doctor alongside a new companion and creative direction, follows this to an extent – we are introduced to Matt Smith's Doctor through a human avatar, with the resolution of the science fiction plot of secondary importance.

In the short term, it's clear that the most important job *Rose* performs is to re-establish **Doctor Who** as a flagship of British popular culture, restoring it to the heart of Saturday evenings and ensuring that the return of the show is not a last, brief hurrah. But with regards to the creative health of the show itself its most important function is in restoring the importance of the companion figure, and making the role no longer subservient to the Doctor, but instead an equal in terms of dramatic possibilities. Leaving aside the often-mooted possibility of a female Doctor, it opens the possibility of a female character driving the show; given that the key moments of the 2005 series mainly belong to Rose and that the

---

[85] The episode *Turn Left* (2008) demonstrates what might happen if the Doctor lacked a companion; with Donna making an alternative decision and never becoming involved in the Racnoss Empress's plan, the Doctor has no moral compass to restrain him and makes a foolhardy mistake resulting in his death. Having a companion can therefore be seen as an act of self-preservation on the Doctor's part.

main overall story is her empowerment, what we get from *Rose* onwards is perhaps more satisfying than a simple change of gender of the lead character. It's human-Time Lord equality and male-female equality, a show actively and satisfyingly modern in both species and gender relations[86], and a show fit for the 21st century.

---

[86] Encouragingly the series has not stood still on this front, but has acknowledged increasingly fluid, non-binary notions of gender in recent seasons, particularly with the character of Missy. For a discussion of this, see Purser-Hallard, Philip, *The Black Archive #4: Dark Water / Death in Heaven*.

CHAPTER 4: 'A GREAT BIG WODGE OF 2005'

'The new series... we want it to be everything the old series was, with a great big wodge of 2005 shoved into it as well.'

[Russell T Davies][87]

When **Doctor Who** is discussed critically there tends to be a category error; it is viewed primarily as a science fiction series, with stories taken in isolation from the contemporary context in which they arose unless the theme and allegory is obvious[88]. It tends to be discussed as an entity in itself, rather than as part of contemporary culture. This error is entirely excusable. **Doctor Who** has largely taken the form of a science fiction series, partly due to the mechanism the titular character uses to travel between adventures. It is, however, too narrow a definition to neatly fit the whole series into – the Hartnell serials set in Earth's past, for instance, contain no science fiction elements bar the TARDIS.

---

[87] **Doctor Who Confidential**, season 1 episode 1, *Bringing Back the Doctor*, BBC3, 26 March 2005.

[88] Examples of obvious parallels being drawn are the Peladon stories of Brian Hayles (*The Curse of Peladon* (1972) and *The Monster of Peladon* (1974)), which respectively use **Doctor Who** to deal with the then contemporary debates over the UK entering the European Union and the political power of miners; the ecological concerns outlined in *The Green Death*; and the satire of Margaret Thatcher's regime in *The Happiness Patrol* (1988). This critical tendency has been reversed recently to some extent by Lawrence Miles and Tat Wood's **About Time** series of critical books, and by historians such as Dominic Sandbrook and Alwyn Turner.

Doctor Who was not originally designed with the priority of making a new science fiction series. Instead it was designed with reference to filling a timeslot in the Saturday evening schedules: a family adventure series which bridged the gap between **Grandstand** (1958-2007) and the likes of **The Telegoons** (1963-64). This description as an adventure series, as per the *Radio Times* capsule description that accompanied each listing in the 1960s, neatly covers the format of all 20th century **Doctor Who** stories and allows its lineage to be traced back through pulp TV fiction, to the likes of the RKO serials such as **Flash Gordon** (1936) and **King of the Rocket Men** (1949), which also used the model of adventure serials punctuated by cliff-hanger endings.

The science fiction label is equally unhelpful when analysing Russell T Davies's vision of **Doctor Who**. Davies taking over **Doctor Who** was, at this point, unique in its history. Serials such as **Queer as Folk**, **Bob and Rose** and **The Second Coming** meant Davies was a critically acclaimed writer; a writer of his stature wanting to work on **Doctor Who** (let alone run the show) was almost unheard of[89]. Davies has recounted how people in the industry asked him what on Earth he was doing it for and asking him 'why waste your time on that sort of thing?'[90] Part of the reason for **Doctor Who**'s return was the BBC wanting Davies to work for them. Because of this it perhaps makes sense to consider Davies's **Doctor Who** in the

---

[89] Although Dennis Potter apparently submitted a script to the **Doctor Who** production office in the 1960s, this was prior to his having established himself.
[90] Davies, Russell T, 'A Long Game'. DWM #359, p33.

context of his career and of the scheduling of the series in prime time on Saturday night.

Davies began his career working in children's television, with stints on **Why Don't You..?** (1973-95) and **On the Waterfront** (1988-9)[91] followed by his first individually-authored series, **Dark Season** (1991) and **Century Falls** (1993). After leaving the BBC he progressed through serial dramas, writing for **Children's Ward** (1989-2000), **Springhill** (1996-97), **Revelations** (1994-96) and **The Grand** (1997-98). To a degree this is a background in what's seen as lowbrow TV: children's drama and soap opera. His career progression came through series which emphasised character to hook viewers, and both his children's work and his time on serial drama are visible influences in *Rose*. Much of the humour in *Rose* arises naturally from the dialogue – the Doctor's response about living shop window dummies trying to take over Britain's shops not being a 'price war', or deflecting a question about his accent with 'lots of planets have a north' – but there is a wide streak of broad humour running through the episode. The Doctor turning down Jackie's seduction, the attack of the Auton arm, the wheelie bin burping after swallowing Mickey, his duplicate absorbing a champagne cork then regurgitating it... this is not sophisticated, Woody Allen wit but more in line with the children's shows Davies had written for, such as **ChuckleVision** (1987-2009), or popular films such as *Dumb and Dumber* (1994) or the **American Pie** series (1999-).

---

[91] He wrote the redubbed dialogue for a comic version of imported French series **The Flashing Blade** (originally **Le Chevalier Tempête**, 1967-69).

Whilst this strain of comedy tends to be frowned on critically, as it relies on humour relating to stupidity or embarrassingly timed bodily functions[92], it's a key part of *Rose*'s appeal. This is a show designed for a popular Saturday night slot, to compete with the populist fare over on ITV (ITV attempted to spike the broadcast of *Rose* with a show presented by its ultimate weapons, perennial light entertainment BAFTA winners Ant and Dec). The lead-in show for Rose on first broadcast was not a drama but **Strictly Come Dancing** spin-off **Strictly Dance Fever** (2005-06)[93], and it led into the game show / lottery draw **The National Lottery: Jet Set** (2001-07). **Doctor Who** is often grouped together with the likes of **Star Trek** (1966-) or **Game of Thrones** (2011-) as popular science fiction or fantasy, but these shows are designed quite differently from **Doctor Who**. The likes of **Star Trek**, **The X-Files** and **Buffy the Vampire Slayer**, other modern shows which are often cited as popular reference points for popular science fiction and fantasy television, were designed as part of a line-up of midweek dramas rather than as part of an entertainment slot[94]. **Doctor Who** can be

---

[92] Rose has a share of this with the wheelie bin which eats Mickey burping; however the 2005 series waits until its fourth episode, *Aliens of London*, for its first fart gag.

[93] Infamously, *Rose*'s first UK broadcast was hampered by a sound feed from the **Strictly Dance Fever** studio accidentally being broadcast over the scene where Rose meets the Autons in the basement.

[94] On the DVD feature 'Doctor Forever – The Unquiet Dead', Davies cites **Lois & Clark: The New Adventures of Superman** (1993-97) as the reference point Jane Tranter and Lorraine Heggessey wanted for a Saturday night fantasy drama. With its decision to focus on the relationship between Clark Kent and Lois Lane as much as

moralistic space opera along the lines of **Star Trek** (for example, *The Mutants* (1972)), it can be conspiracy drama such as **The X-Files** (*The Impossible Astronaut / Day of the Moon* (2011)) or it can play around with contemporary takes on mythological monsters like **Buffy** (*The Abominable Snowmen* (1967), *The Vampires of Venice* (2010), *Mummy on the Orient Express* (2014), or much of the early Tom Baker era under the auspices of Philip Hinchcliffe and Robert Holmes).

This misapprehension has not been confined to fans; arguably many of the problems in **Doctor Who**'s history have arisen when it has produced material unsuitable for its timeslot – whilst the episodes produced under Hinchcliffe and Holmes remain popular with fans (accounting for eight of the top 25 spots in *Doctor Who Magazine*'s 50th anniversary poll)[95], and in terms of ratings, their version of **Doctor Who** drew complaints from the puritanical Mary Whitehouse and her National Viewers and Listeners Association[96]. Hinchcliffe was abruptly moved on to what was considered a more suitable programme, the adult police drama **Target** (1977-78), and his successor, Graham Williams, told to tone down the violence and horror. Similarly, in the 1980s Peter Davison's three seasons as the Doctor had their content dictated to a degree by a weekday

---

Superman's exploits it is, tonally, the most direct genre antecedent of Davies's **Doctor Who**.

[95] 'Doctor Who: The First 50 Years'. DWM #474. This easily outstrips any other era of the show, including the combined output under Russell T Davies and Steven Moffat, a remarkable feat for episodes broadcast almost 40 years earlier.

[96] Whitehouse had complained about Doctor Who before, including Autons disguising themselves as policemen.

timeslot and were able to deal with more adult material[97], but when the show was moved back to a Saturday timeslot for Season 22 an unchanged approach to violence was frowned upon[98]. Tonally, for an early Saturday evening slot traditionally devoted to light entertainment, incidents such as Lytton's hands being squeezed to a bloody pulp in *Attack of the Cybermen*, the Doctor's quip following two guards falling into an acid bath in *Vengeance on Varos* and Shockeye knifing Oscar in *The Two Doctors* (all 1985) felt even more out of place than they might have done in the early evening slot of the Davison years.

Davies is far too savvy as a writer to make the mistakes of his forebears; he is well aware that he is writing for an early Saturday night slot, and the tone of the drama it requires. He is not incapable of writing a version of **Doctor Who** aimed squarely at adults – his 1996 **New Adventures** novel *Damaged Goods* is a bleak portrait of life on a council estate in 1987 which involves drug

---

[97] Script editor Eric Saward's approach was naturally bleak; in a weekday slot the show could get away with the high body count of *Resurrection of the Daleks*, and the gunfights between gunrunners and troopers in *The Caves of Androzani*. *Androzani* also included scenes of Stotz, the mercenary leader, almost forcing his subordinate Krelper to swallow a poison pill, plenty of shootings and Sharaz Jek strangling his enemy Morgus and forcing his head into a machine.

[98] The actual presentation of violent actions in stories such as *Attack of the Cybermen*, *Vengeance on Varos* and *The Two Doctors* is largely in line with what we see in *Resurrection of the Daleks* and *The Caves of Androzani*; however, the sixth Doctor's lack of empathy compared to his previous incarnation means the acts are set in the context of a darker show.

abuse, cottaging, the Doctor's companion sleeping with another man, plenty of bodily horror and, for good measure, gratuitous continuity with the plot revolving around an ancient Gallifreyan superweapon. In tonal terms it's absolutely unlike anything of the episodes of the show he oversees; it would be 18-rated and, without extensive rewrites, unbroadcastable before the watershed. Yet it is perfectly in keeping with the tone of that series, which was aimed at a fan audience numbered in the thousands rather than a mass audience numbered in millions, and where drug abuse, violence and companions having a sex life were not uncommon[99].

Rose shares a number of similarities with *Damaged Goods*, such as a council estate setting, but the presentation of the story is very different; lighter, broader and with more comedy. Where *Damaged Goods* rubs the reader's face in the horror of council estate life in 1987, *Rose* tones this down to drudgery, the daily grind of ordinariness. It's about someone getting by to the point of having lost sight of a wider world, rather than someone suffering deprivation and depravity; as callous as it might sound, the latter would be too depressing for the timeslot. It exposes the disconnection between what the fan audience and the mass audience want: the fan audience generally prefer a programme with a darker tone that can be taken seriously as a drama; the mass audience simply want an entertaining programme for a Saturday night. The two are not necessarily mutually exclusive; **Doctor**

---

[99] One book, Kate Orman's *The Left-Handed Hummingbird*, featured the Doctor taking LSD, and was combined with Sylvester McCoy being in a play featuring nudity to attempt to whip up a headline about the unhealthy moral state of **Doctor Who**.

Who's format is flexible enough to contain a darker tone (as *Dalek* proves later in the season), but with its inherent 'Saturday nightness' it would be unhealthy for it to be consistently dark. Certainly it would have been a mistake for **Doctor Who** to have attempted to be a serious science fiction drama, a genre with limited appeal compared to the wide audience the show was being aimed at.

Instead *Rose* deliberately starts out as a normal contemporary drama series, concealing the science fiction aspect until Rose and the domestic aspects of her life have been established. The only hint that this is a science fiction show (aside from the **Doctor Who** brand) is the opening shot being a zoom from space, quietly indicating that the show's concerns are greater than simply modern urban life. The first few minutes are deliberately mundane; Rose waking up to her alarm going off, saying goodbye to her mum, going to work and messing about with her boyfriend on her lunch break. On the DVD commentary for *Rose*, Davies notes that this is entirely deliberate; he doesn't want to give casual viewers a reason to turn off by explicitly giving them a science fiction show straight away. This is in line with his overall philosophy of giving the show firm roots in 2005; Rose has her own time to go back to if she wishes, and in its first year back the show ventures no further from the Earth than a couple of space stations in Earth orbit.

The influence of other genres on Davies's version of **Doctor Who** are not limited to the shows he wrote for. The structure of the show is also influenced by shows contemporary to the period when Davies was devising the structure of the show. Davies is on record as admiring **Buffy the Vampire Slayer**[100], and from this show he borrowed the idea of a series arc based around character. Shows such as **Babylon 5** and **The X-Files** had pioneered the idea of arc stories but had spread them across multiple seasons and largely based them on plot rather than character; however, **Babylon 5**'s uncertain existence resulted in its dramatic arc being compromised[101] and SF conspiracy show **Dark Skies** (1996-97)'s planned five-year arc was cut short, unresolved after one. Far better to have a story lasting for one year that did not depend on the memory of events of past years[102]; this protects against the possibility of stories being left uncompleted, in the event of the show being cancelled. Davies explained his rationale for concentrating on character ahead of plot by comparing **Star Trek** and **Buffy**:

---

[100] '...I loved what Joss Whedon did with **Buffy The Vampire Slayer**, obviously.' (Bahn, Christopher, 'TV Club Interview: Russell T Davies'.)

[101] The story of humanity's civil war was foreshortened, with a subplot designed to take up less time regarding the telepaths on Babylon 5 leading a revolt then brought to the fore. As a result, the first half of the final season feels flat compared to the earlier seasons of the show.

[102] This may also be influenced by soap operas. Gareth Roberts in 'We're gonna be bigger than Star Wars' feature recalls a **Coronation Street** writer telling him that 'anything that happened over six months ago is ancient history'. Whilst the number of episodes of soap operas per year is vastly larger than other dramas, the point stands that a mass audience will not generally be engaged enough to recall finer points of continuity.

'...there's so much potential in science fiction, but you read the listings magazine and under **Star Trek: Enterprise** it'll say, "The Crystals of Poffnar have been hidden in a cave, and so-and-so argues with the Federation that they have to be retrieved". What is there to watch in that?! But one of **Buffy**'s billings might be, "Buffy falls in love and discovers he's a monster." Brilliant! It speaks to your heart. That's a great model to follow. It's the emotion they get in there, the fun they have.'[103]

Davies's model of drama is fundamentally based on people being interested in people rather than ideas; that they will watch something that emotionally engages them, rather than for the ideas presented. As with the element of broad humour, this is not something that tends to garner critical praise; there is, after all, little critical mileage in decoding why something has bypassed the rational brain and stimulated emotions. It's why, musically, critics tended to favour Blur over Oasis during the Britpop era – whereas the former had an obvious intellectual element to their work, including social critique and a willingness to experiment musically, the latter tended to favour connecting through familiarity (often to the point of plagiarism); big gestures over considered moments. In this case what matters is the connection the material makes with the audience; Noel Gallagher has often derided his lyrics as being about nothing, meaningless when written but when '...there's a 15-year old kid, he's got his top off and he's singing it, crying his eyes

---

103 Davies, Russell T, 'Tooth and Claw'. DWM #360, pp13-14.

out and I'm thinking "That's what it's about."'[104]. Davies is capable of clever, subtle writing but his approach to a Saturday night television programme is similar to Gallagher's songwriting: to emotionally connect with the audience through a spectacle of the form, prioritising emotional meaning over explicit meaning. The grand sweep is more important than the detail. In both cases they want to make you care even if you don't understand why, bypassing the head to get to the heart[105].

The other element which feeds into the season's arc story is the reality television genre which became popular in the early 21st century. Davies is a vociferous advocate for reality TV – he has defended it as storytelling and even described an incident from the first series of **Big Brother** (2000-) as 'the best bit of drama transmitted' in the previous five or six years[106]. His fondness for the genre, along with his affection for makeover shows and game shows, is most overtly evident in the macabre parodies of them

---

[104] Bilmes, Alex, 'The stage was set. And we turned up. And the people said "Yes." And then it just exploded', *Esquire*, p157.
[105] For further discussion of this topic with relation to music see Carl Wilson's *Let's Talk About Love: Why Other People Have Such Bad Taste* and with regard to arts in general John Carey's *What Good Are the Arts?*.
[106] O'Brien, Steve and Nick Setchfield, 'Russell Spouts', *SFX Collection Doctor Who Past! Present! Future!*, Future Publishing, 2005, p39. The incident involved contestant Nick Bateman attempting to manipulate eviction nominations from fellow housemates, against the series rules, and being confronted about it by other housemates led by Craig Phillips. The incident is available to view on YouTube at
https://www.youtube.com/watch?v=ri01fflx.

presented in *Bad Wolf*. However, the structure of Rose's arc is drawn from the talent show subgenre, particularly series such as **The X Factor** (2004-). These shows begin with audition weeks, where the general public turn up to a series of events across the country to get on the show. The hopeful contestants who pass the auditions then sing each week, with the public's two least favourite performances being forced to sing against each other and the contestant judged the worst being voted off the show. The format lends itself to repeated moments of high drama with the moment of voting-off, previously favoured contestants dropping into the bottom two and judges who express negative critical opinions becoming pantomime villains. The story of winning contestants is packaged in the final episode as a series of highlights to represent the trials they've survived and their progress through the series (often described as a 'journey').

Rose's 'journey' roughly follows this model, *Rose* itself being the audition phase of the show, with Rose's morals and willingness to hold the Doctor to account meaning she passes the companion audition, and the climactic moment of drama being her acceptance onto the show.[107] The first season proceeds to broadly follow the model of the reality show storyline – *The End of the World*, *The Unquiet Dead* and *Aliens of London / World War Three* show her being taught about the wider universe and what the role of companion might entail. It can even be said that these stories involve 'celebrity' tutors to aid the process; the 'last human'

---

[107] The idea of the Doctor auditioning his companions through a similar process to that used in talent shows was explicitly parodied in the Big Finish audio drama *Situation Vacant* (2010).

Cassandra, Charles Dickens and future Prime Minister Harriet Jones. *Dalek* and *The Long Game* serve to contrast her with someone far less suitable to being the Doctor's companion; Adam's flaws serving to underline Rose's contrasting virtues and why she's so suitable to continue travelling with the Doctor. *The Long Game* itself can be seen as a failed audition; what might have happened to Rose if she had not proven so suitable. *Father's Day* serves as the equivalent of Rose's trial; her falling into the bottom two, with the serious misstep of altering time by saving her father from death almost seeing her leave the show. *Boom Town* underlines how much the process has changed her character; with Mickey, who has remained behind, clearly somewhat alienated by how her travels with the Doctor have changed her. Her ascendancy to effective godhood in *The Parting of the Ways* is the equivalent to becoming the victorious contestant; her potential being realised in the way **The X Factor** sees a number one hit as potential being realised.

The influence of pop culture on Davies's version of **Doctor Who** is not limited to structure, but is also explicit within the text. **Doctor Who** had rarely directly embraced other pop culture icons in its 20th-century incarnation. The Beatles make an appearance in *The Chase*, their 'Paperback Writer' can be heard in the background of *The Evil of the Daleks* (1967) and they're quoted in *The Three Doctors* (1972-73); there's a vague allusion to Jimmy Savile in *The War Machines* (1966), Fleetwood Mac can be heard in *Spearhead From Space* and the Master listens to King Crimson in The Mind of Evil (1971), but otherwise the series studiously avoids the pop culture icons of the day. Indeed, 'An Unearthly Child' invents a band rather than play a contemporary record[108] and Ace, supposedly a streetwise teenager, reveals an unlikely fondness for jazz records. *Revelation of the Daleks* (1985) and *Remembrance of the Daleks* feature old records, but the former is deliberately nostalgic and the latter is to provide period detail.

This is partly a function of the series spending large amounts of time away from contemporary Earth, but more because pop culture seems unimportant in any way to the lead characters. Ian and Barbara are familiar with the Beatles, but given the chance they're far more interested in what Shakespeare and Lincoln got up to. Of the remaining companions, only Ben and Polly are grounded in the culture of their day, being seen to frequent a nightclub, and few display any popular interests (Yates and Benton watch rugby union in *The Dæmons* (1971), the Master watches **The Clangers** (1969-72) for the sake of a joke in *The Sea Devils* (1972) and Ace demonstrates support for Charlton Athletic in *Silver Nemesis*). Characters in the 20th-century series, whether from contemporary Earth or not, are rarely given any hinterland beyond that which they need to have to fulfil their plot function. We don't know what Polly and Ben listened to, what Sarah Jane watched when she went home at night or what Tegan might have read for amusement[109] – or even if they did any of those things. Most of what we know of

---

[108] 'John Smith and the Common Men'. (Although given 'John Smith' is the stage name of the Honourable Aubrey Waites it's debatable how common they were.)

[109] In the **Doctor Who Missing Adventures** novel *Goth Opera*, Paul Cornell suggests that Tegan reads Primo Levi for fun. It's a wonderfully unlikely idea.

companions is defined by their family, occupations or qualifications, or lack of the same, elements that help the writers by defining a set of abilities rather than character. Any idea we have of what they're like as people is entirely in the actor's performance or an odd throwaway line that helps the story along. **Doctor Who** stories were dated by their production, not their contemporary references.

With Davies keen to root the new series in the modern day, this changes. Davies once again bypasses the type of culture likely to be critically acclaimed in favour of genuinely popular mass culture. Jackie's flat does not contain unlikely highbrow literature; instead the Doctor finds a copy of the celebrity gossip magazine *Heat* (cracking a joke which indicates a familiarity with these magazines) and a copy of the bestselling *The Lovely Bones* (2002). Both *Heat* and *The Lovely Bones* were publications which sold very well in 2005; the type of literature people were actually reading as opposed to what it was considered they should be reading. This continues with the use of pop music in *The End of the World*, with the use of Soft Cell's 'Tainted Love' and Britney Spears 'Toxic' as 'classical music from humanity's greatest composers'. Whilst this direct use of popular culture is something that helps convince the audience that this is a plausible simulacrum of our world, the increased contemporary references also mean that these episodes date faster than stories from the old series; what anchors it for the people who watched *Rose* or *The End of the World* on first broadcast will mean relatively little to those coming to it later. This version of **Doctor Who** also uses culture visually; it's aware of the power of the alien set against an iconic location in the way the old series was when showing the Daleks in London in *The Dalek Invasion of Earth* (1964) or the Cybermen walking down the steps of St Paul's Cathedral in *The Invasion* (1968)[110]. It's again used to give the viewer reassuring signs that this is a world they could be familiar with and also to provide iconic imagery – in *Rose* the London Eye is the prime example of this, being incorporated into the Auton invasion plan and essentially turned into a giant transmitter. As Davies puts it on the DVD commentary, **Doctor Who**'s '...unique quality is to take everyday things and make them scary'. The use of the London Eye does this on a grand scale (as does the damage to Big Ben in *Aliens of London*), but it also applies on a smaller scale with the use of common objects such as shop window dummies and wheelie bins as part of an invasion scheme – it takes not only the grand, iconic features of everyday urban landscape and twists them, but common, mundane ones too.

The other changing feature which marks *Rose* out from 20th century **Doctor Who** is that it directly tackles the way mass media has changed in the intervening years. It's the first episode of **Doctor Who** of the internet era, and thus the first to acknowledge that it exists. Whilst there was a relatively small community of internet users in 1996[111], globally measured in millions, by 2005 over half of UK households had an internet connection[112]. Rose's use of a search engine to help track the Doctor down is again something

---

[110] Jon Pertwee pithily summed up the incongruity as 'a Yeti on the loo in Tooting Bec.' (*Myth Makers: Jon Pertwee*).

[111] Roughly 1.3% of the world's population according to 'Internet Users', Internet Live.

[112] Data from the Office for National Statistics.

that roots the series in the familiar[113]. Similarly the destruction of Henrik's is covered by the BBC News channel; we are in the age of 24 hour news. This is entirely new territory for **Doctor Who**, where previous versions of the show tended to assume that alien invasions had managed to escape the notice of the general population to an almost ludicrous degree[114]. Davies's version acknowledges that the degree of secrecy posited by 20th-century **Doctor Who** would be near impossible in 2005. This is something that will be addressed even more directly in *Aliens of London / World War Three*, with the arrival of the fake spaceship covered on the news removing plausible deniability about the existence of alien life. In the long term this works against Davies's populist instinct; there is only a limited amount of time in which a world which is repeatedly invaded can remain relatable to for audiences. By the time Davies departs, the Earth of **Doctor Who** is a far different place from our own; not only has there been a worldwide fight between Daleks and Cybermen but at different points the whole planet has been dragged through space and virtually the entire world's population was briefly transformed into the Master, most of it documented on news channels. To resolve this credibility

---

[113] It also serves to date the episode fairly precisely in that Rose needs to drop round and use Mickey's computer. These days she'd be able to google the Doctor from her phone.

[114] *Remembrance of the Daleks* even cracks a joke about this, with Ace asking the Doctor why she's never heard of a 1963 Dalek invasion and the Doctor responding with a list of invasions and a dig at the human capacity for self-deception. A similar gag features in *The Runaway Bride* with Donna, who simply wasn't paying attention when the planet was invaded.

issue, Steven Moffat was forced to reboot the universe at the end of his first season. Again, it's indicative that for Davies's version of **Doctor Who** to remain true to itself as rooted in the recognisable, it had a relatively short shelf life before the weight of internal logic caused its plausibility to collapse.

Rose, ultimately, is the correction of the category error of the 1980s. John Nathan-Turner was often derided by fans for his populist instincts, for stunts such as having Beryl Reid cast as a spaceship captain[115], finding roles for comedians such as Alexei Sayle and Hale and Pace, or casting Bonnie Langford as a companion. This ignores the fact that **Doctor Who** had resorted to such casting on several occasions in its past, with Peter Glaze and Bernard Bresslaw appearing as aliens and John Cleese and Eleanor Bron making entirely gratuitous cameo appearances in *City of Death* (1979). The desire of much of fandom to have a show that they could take seriously, and that would not get them laughed at by their peers, blinded them to the fact that their favourite show was popular entertainment and that the stories they praised and wanted more of – the likes of *Earthshock* or *The Caves of Androzani* (1984) – were in fact outliers in terms of **Doctor Who**'s history. These shows were excellent examples of **Doctor Who**, but they were ultimately taken as a template for the show, particularly for season 22 which emphasised action, violence and gruesome

---

[115] Writer Eric Saward originally envisaged the role that went to Reid as a standard male spaceship captain. Peter Grimwade's reversal of a gender-stereotypical role is one of the best things about *Earthshock*; it makes what would be a largely forgettable role into a memorably entertaining one.

deaths. That season was an example of fans getting what they wanted and ultimately not liking it, the mordant instincts of Saward completely overriding any populism injected by Nathan-Turner. Even the Andrew Cartmel creative revival took its cues mainly from a minority interest; the comic *2000AD* and particularly the Alan Moore story *The Ballad of Halo Jones* (1984-86).

Rose demonstrates that to make popular Saturday night television it's a good idea to let populist instincts rule: to embrace casting that might bring good publicity, to acknowledge the wider world and to draw your storytelling cues from contemporaries[116]. Russell T Davies's great revolution was to take **Doctor Who**, a show once about the future but which had been living in the past, and to make it a show of the moment, one which sought to capture the zeitgeist of 2005. To seize that moment it needed to acknowledge how times had changed, that it would need to be modern not only in terms of format and the technicalities of production, but in terms of the characters and culture it presented. And of the potential candidates to revive the show none was as well suited as Davies to provide this revolution.

Doctor Who was the popular show which ended up charming the unusual children looking for a more intellectual breed of hero who generally solved his problems with his wits rather than fists or bombs. But the perception of it as for outsiders was a retrospective imposition of the 1980s, when the cool kids were coveting David

---

[116] For instance, it may or may not be coincidence that the season finale, *The Parting of the Ways*, shares a title with the penultimate chapter of J K Rowling's *Harry Potter and the Goblet of Fire*.

Hasselhoff's intelligent car in **Knight Rider** (1982-86), thrilling to the latest shoot-'em-up in **The A-Team** (1983-87) or marvelling at the spectacle of the **Star Wars** films (1977-) that **Doctor Who** simply could not match on a shoestring budget. Davies's version of **Doctor Who** is not aimed at outsiders; that would have been a short-lived revival indeed. Instead he trusted his popular instincts, ones honed from his lifelong addiction to television[117]. Davies's goal was to restore **Doctor Who** to the heart of popular culture, to aim it like a TV blunderbuss at as wide an audience as possible. To make it watercooler television that was being talked about in workplaces, on internet forums and in national newspapers.

Anecdotal evidence from my office in the week of the broadcast of *The Parting of the Ways* indicated that he succeeded beyond his wildest dreams, with several people desperate to try and find out how the cliff-hanger from *Bad Wolf* was resolved. Before *Rose* was broadcast **Doctor Who** fandom was seen as slightly strange, a devotion to a long-dormant show. After *Rose* the show was no longer for the outsiders. It seized the moment - perhaps less strange than it had been before, but finally sitting at the heart of pop culture in a way it hadn't since the 1970s.

---

[117] According to Mark Aldridge and Andy Murray's 2009 biography of *Russell T Davies: T is for Television – The Authorised Screen Biography*, when the crew of **Bob and Rose** used Davies's house as a base for shooting, Alan Davies incurred Davies' wrath by actually turning the TV off (Davies claimed he didn't know it actually had an off switch).

CONCLUSION: 'NO-ONE EXPECTED THAT. NO-ONE.'

On his last night in Cardiff, at the suggestion of Ben Cook, his co-author on *The Writer's Tale*, Russell T Davies sat down to watch *Rose*. He had, at this point, spent nearly six years writing and show-running **Doctor Who**. It was essentially a victory lap; a reminder of how things had gone so right in 2005. *Rose* had suffered a few mishaps – a rough cut of the episode was leaked onto the internet three weeks before transmission, a sound feed from **Strictly Come Dancing** leaked across the scene where Rose first encounters the Autons, and within days of broadcast it was announced that Christopher Eccleston would be leaving the role after only one season – but ultimately it accomplished its aim of resurrecting **Doctor Who** perfectly. It was watched by 10.8 million viewers and received an Audience Appreciation index score of 81; an indication that the show had a rare combination of a mass audience and popular acclaim.

By the end of the year the show had consistently maintained that combination, and the 2005 season picked up awards from the viewing audience (Eccleston and Piper collecting the 2005 National TV Awards for Most Popular Actor and Actress and the show collecting Most Popular Drama), the industry (winning the 2006 Best Drama BAFTA) and the fan community (the nominated episodes of the show filling the top three slots in the 2006 Hugo Awards' Best Dramatic Presentation, Short Form category[118]). **Doctor Who** was unquestionably the television success story of the

---

[118] *The Empty Child* beat *Dalek* and *Father's Day*.

year, popular enough to be awarded a Christmas Day episode. In 2007 the episode *Voyage of the Damned* was the second most watched programme on television all year, beaten only by the Christmas day episode of **EastEnders** (1985-). And at the end of its fourth season, with the episode *Journey's End* (2008), **Doctor Who** achieved the distinction of being the most watched show in the UK that week. These were achievements that even the previous popularity highpoints of Dalekmania and the Jon Pertwee and Tom Baker eras could not match. Russell T Davies' iteration is, by the metrics of ratings, awards and audience appreciation, the most popular version of **Doctor Who** in history. If **Doctor Who** has what Neil Tennant has called an imperial phase[119], the era curated by Russell T Davies is that phase[120] – a remarkable achievement for a 42-year-old show that had produced one episode in the 16 years preceding *Rose*.

---

[119] Tennant coined the term in relation to pop music, the idea being that a band has a phase in its career where it peaks critically and commercially and can essentially take any creative risks it wishes to (cited on p257 of Harris, John, *The Last Party: Britpop, Blair and the Demise of English Rock*). His Pet Shop Boys' bandmate Chris Lowe summed it up more succinctly: 'It means you can do what you like, usually followed by disappearing up your backside' (quoted in Tom Ewing, 'Imperial').

[120] **Doctor Who** is a remarkable cultural artefact in having at least three such phases; the initial popularity fuelled by Dalekmania; the mid-70s period covered by the producerships of Barry Letts and Philip Hinchcliffe; and the era overseen by Russell T Davies. Arguably its increased international success under Steven Moffat constitutes another such phase. The show's very continued existence and success is a rebuttal of the concept of 'jumping the shark'.

Rose is the foundation stone of that achievement. Upon re-watching Davies was 'amazed' that 'so much of what I wanted from **Doctor Who** was so present and clear, from the opening titles onwards'[121]. In a show that thrives on change he put the show's success down to finding a successful formula and sticking to it:

> '...this show is exactly what I wanted it to be, and it is, in its first 45 minutes, exactly what it is now. It has never fundamentally changed.'[122]

> 'The show has driven more and more people to it as time has gone on, and it hasn't increased its audience by changing; it's done so by staying the same, by being consistent, by never flinching.'[123]

In a collaborative medium such as television auteur theory is a nonsense; it's impossible for one person to control everything, including acting choices, direction, costumes and scripts. But the show overseen by Russell T Davies comes close. With *Rose*, Davies finds a new, modern formula for how to tell a **Doctor Who** story: fast-paced 45-minute dramas which prioritise character over plot mechanics. *Rose* deconstructs **Doctor Who**, questioning what the absolute fundamentals of the show are, stripping the show back to those fundamentals and using what's left to refit the series into a style very much dictated by Davies.

---

[121] Davies, Russell T, and Benjamin Cook, *The Writer's Tale: The Final Chapter*, p685.
[122] Davies and Cook, *The Writer's Tale* p682.
[123] Davies and Cook, *The Writer's Tale* p685.

This is arguably as close as **Doctor Who** will ever come to having an auteur behind it, with a recognisably distinctive style of writing and absolute attention to every detail of production[124]. In an earlier era of television, Davies might well have been an even more populist version of Dennis Potter, producing one-off plays and miniseries[125]. The comparison with Potter is not a facile one; both Davies and Potter were great believers in the democratic power of television, both with 'a desire to communicate beyond a narrow cultural elite'[126]. Potter explained his choice of career as a television writer by the fact that, due to '…the accidents of technical innovation, we are now in a situation where a writer can communicate to more people in more open circumstances than has hitherto been possible'[127]. Davies's omnivorous appetite for television means that he is perhaps more instinctively a television writer than Potter, but his instinctive decisions about what would make for good, populist

---

[124] This attention may come from foundations laid by Davies, but is also enforced by his fellow producers Julie Gardner and Phil Collinson.

[125] **Doctor Who** and its spin-offs are arguably the exceptions rather than the rules in Davies's career since the success of **Queer as Folk**. His output has consisted mainly of short-run series: **Bob and Rose**, **The Second Coming**, **Mine All Mine**, **Casanova** (2005), **Cucumber** and **Banana** (both 2015). In further parallels with Potter, both produced versions of **Casanova** (Potter's in 1971), and both produced works that questioned Christianity (Davies with **The Second Coming** and Potter with *Son of Man* (1969), *Brimstone and Treacle* (1976) and *Angels Are So Few* (1970)).

[126] Williams, John 'Introduction' to Potter, Dennis, *The Art of Invective: Selected Non-Fiction 1953-1994*, ebook location 720.

[127] Potter, *The Art of Invective*, ebook location 2897.

95

television demonstrates that he is equally as aware of its potentialities as Potter[128]. His awareness of how a popular drama series can shape attitudes is visible in the way alternative sexualities are treated as normal and healthy in the series[129]. It is equally rewarding to analyse his version of **Doctor Who** as part of his career as it is as part of the show's history; the success of the show is down in equal parts to the potential of the **Doctor Who** format and to Davies's style.

The success of *Rose* was not limited to the direct effect of restoring **Doctor Who** to the timeslot it was designed for. As well as the series inspiring three spin-offs[130], it briefly changed the nature of Saturday night television; in the wake of **Doctor Who**'s success both major channels searched for further successful Saturday night

---

[128] Frank Cottrell Boyce (who would later write the 2014 episode *In the Forest of the Night*) argues that this is a result of Davies's own tastes meeting his artistic sensibilities: 'Russell's magic is that he has genuinely populist tastes – he loves a good Saturday night – but he also has the courage and ambition of an artist. It's a Damon Albarn, Stevie Wonder, Hergé like quality.' Aldridge and Murray, *Russell T Davies,* p 224.

[129] This was termed a 'gay agenda', and Davies has admitted the promotion of homosexuality and bisexuality as normal and healthy was quite deliberate.

[130] As well as **Torchwood** (2006-11), **The Sarah Jane Adventures** (2007-11) and **Class** (projected to begin in 2016), at least two further series were proposed. CBBC expressed an interest in making a series about the adventures of a young Doctor, and **Rose Tyler: Earth Defence** was cancelled at a late stage, Davies considering it a 'spin-off too far' and that it would spoil the parent show (Cook, Benjamin, 'Brave New Worlds', DWM #373, p31.

action-adventure formats; ITV had **Primeval**, a time-travelling show heavily featuring a former pop star, and the BBC have attempted to complement **Doctor Who** several times with **Robin Hood, Merlin** and **Atlantis**. All were reasonable successes, running for multiple seasons, but none quite captured the success of **Doctor Who**.

As a story, *Rose*'s reputation has waned during the years; it was critically eclipsed by episodes such as *The Empty Child / The Doctor Dances* (2005), *Bad Wolf / The Parting of the Ways, Human Nature / The Family of Blood* (2007) and *Blink* (2007) in the Davies era alone, and in ratings terms and BARB chart positions by the likes of *The Christmas Invasion, Voyage of the Damned* and *Journey's End*. In the light of the revival of **Doctor Who** lasting beyond a decade and with a secure long-term future[131], it's easy to forget what a remarkable episode *Rose* is and the impact it made. It brings one of the most critically-acclaimed writers of the time to the show and allows him to set out his vision of what **Doctor Who** can be. It sets out to take **Doctor Who** from being a television museum piece to a modern, dynamic show, to introduce it to new viewers whilst deliberately not alienating the fan audience. It takes the possibilities of character-led drama, largely unexplored by the 20th-century version of **Doctor Who**, and adds them to the storytelling possibilities of the show. It brings **Doctor Who** into the era of CGI, where effects work can finally match the imaginative power of its writers. It provides the impetus for the producers of British

---

[131] 'It is definitely going to last five more years, I've seen the business plan. It's not going anywhere. And I think we can go past that. It's television's own legend. It will just keep going.' (Vivarelli, 'Lucca Comics'.)

network television to rethink their ideas about what might work in a Saturday night schedule. It realises the chameleonic potential of **Doctor Who** to change as television changes, to reflect the state of popular culture and the way television is made[132]. And it does all this whilst remaining true to the essential nature of the show, the simple joy of a Time Lord and a companion having fantastic adventures in space and time.

It remains, in the wider context of its achievements, one of the most remarkable pieces of television made in the UK this century.

> 'And she runs. Rose's POV: rushing top speed towards the blue box. And she's never been so happy – CU Rose running as the almighty shriek of the cliffhanger music scorches in and accelerates her through the door...
>
> 'Into adventure.'
>
> ['Rose', *Doctor Who: The Shooting Scripts*][133]

---

[132] In the *Variety* interview Steven Moffat described it as 'the all-time perfectly evolved television show', a 'television predator' (Vivarelli, 'Lucca Comics').

[133] Davies, *The Shooting Scripts* p47.

BIBLIOGRAPHY

Books

Aaronovitch, Ben, *Remembrance of the Daleks*. **Doctor Who: The New Adventures**. London, WH Allen, 1990. ISBN 9780426203372.

Aldridge, Mark, and Andy Murray, *Russell T Davies: T Is for Television – The Authorised Screen Biography*. Richmond, Reynolds & Hearn Ltd, 2008. ISBN 9781905287840.

Carey, John, *What Good Are the Arts?* London, Faber and Faber, 2005. ISBN 9780571226023.

Cartmel, Andrew, *Cat's Cradle: Warhead*. **Doctor Who: The New Adventures**. London, Virgin Publishing Ltd, 1992. ISBN 9780426203674.

Cartmel, Andrew, *Warlock*. **Doctor Who: The New Adventures**. London, Virgin Publishing Ltd, 1995. ISBN 9780426204336.

Cartmel, Andrew, *Warchild*. **Doctor Who: The New Adventures**. London, Virgin Publishing Ltd, 1996. ISBN 9780426204640.

Cartmel, Andrew, *Through Time: An Unauthorised and Unofficial History of Doctor Who*. London, Bloomsbury Academic, 2005. ISBN 9780826417329.

Chapman, James, *Inside the TARDIS: The Worlds of Doctor Who – A Cultural History*. London, I B Tauris, 2006. ISBN 9781845111632.

Cole, Stephen, *The Monsters Inside*. London, BBC Books, 2005. ISBN 9780563486299.

Cooray Smith, James, *The Massacre*. **The Black Archive** #2. Edinburgh, Obverse Books, 2016. ISBN 9781909031388.

Cornell, Paul, *Timewyrm: Revelation*. **Doctor Who: The New Adventures**. London, Virgin Publishing Ltd, 1991. ISBN 9780426203605.

Cornell, Paul, *Goth Opera*. **Doctor Who: The Missing Adventures**. London, Virgin Publishing Ltd, 1994. ISBN 9780426204183.

Cornell, Paul (ed), *Licence Denied: Rumblings from the Doctor Who Underground*. London, Virgin Publishing Ltd, 1997. ISBN 978073501047.

Davies, Russell T, *Damaged Goods*. **Doctor Who: The New Adventures**. London, Virgin Publishing Ltd, 1996. ISBN 9780426204831.

Davies, Russell T, et al, *Doctor Who: The Shooting Scripts*. London, BBC Books, 2005. ISBN 9780563486411.

Davies, Russell T, and Benjamin Cook, *The Writer's Tale: The Final Chapter*. London, BBC Books, 2010. ISBN 9781846078613.

Dicks, Terrance, *The Eight Doctors*. **Doctor Who: The Eighth Doctor Adventures**. London, BBC Books, 1997. ISBN 9780563405635.

Harris, John, *The Last Party: Britpop, Blair and the Demise of English Rock*. London, 4th Estate, 2003. ISBN 978000713472X.

Howe, David J, Mark Stammers and Stephen James Walker, *Doctor Who: The Sixties*. London, Virgin Publishing, 1992. ISBN 9781852274204.

Howe, David J, Mark Stammers and Stephen James Walker, *The First Doctor*. **Doctor Who: The Handbook**. London, Virgin Publishing, 1994. ISBN 9780426204301.

Howe, David J, and Stephen James Walker, *Doctor Who: The Television Companion*. London, BBC Books, 1998. ISBN 9780563405887.

Letts, Barry, *Who & Me: The Memoir Of Barry Letts, Doctor Who Producer 1969-1974*. King's Lynn, Fantom Films, 2009. ISBN 9781906263447.

Lofficier, Jean-Marc, *Doctor Who: The Terrestrial Index*. London, Virgin Publishing Ltd, 1991. ISBN 9780426203612.

Lyon, J Shaun, *Back to the Vortex*. Tolworth, Telos Publishing, 2005. ISBN 9781903889787.

Magrs, Paul, *The Diary of a Doctor Who Addict*. London, Simon and Schuster, 2010. ISBN 9781847284126.

Miles, Lawrence, and Tat Wood, *1975-1979: Seasons 12-17*. **About Time: The Unauthorised Guide to Doctor Who**. Des Moines, Mad Norwegian Press, 2004. ISBN 9780975944639.

Miller, Frank, *The Dark Night Returns*. DC Comics, 1986. London, Titan Books, 1997. ISBN 9781852867980.

Moore, Alan, and Dave Gibbons, *Watchmen*. DC Comics, 1986-87. New York, DC Comics, 1987. ISBN 9780930289232.

Moore, Alan, and Ian Gibson, *The Complete Ballad of Halo Jones*. *2000 AD*, 1984-86. Oxford, Rebellion, 2007. ISBN 9781905437184.

Niven, Larry, 'Man of Steel, Woman of Kleenex'. Published in Niven, Larry, *All the Myriad Ways*. New York, Ballantine Books, 1971. ISBN 9780345022806.

Orman, Kate, *The Left-Handed Hummingbird*. **Doctor Who: The New Adventures**. London, Virgin Publishing Ltd, 1993. ISBN 9780426204046.

Orman, Kate, *The Year of Intelligent Tigers*. **Doctor Who: The Eighth Doctor Adventures**. London, BBC Books, 2001. ISBN 9780563538318.

Parkin, Lance, *The Dying Days*. **Doctor Who: The New Adventures**. London, Virgin Publishing, 1997. ISBN 9780563538318.

Parkin, Lance, and Lars Pearson, *Ahistory: An Unauthorised History of the Doctor Who Universe*. 3rd edition. Des Moines, Mad Norwegian Press, 2012. ISBN 9781935234111.

Potter, Dennis, *The Art of Invective: Selected Non-Fiction 1953-1994*. Ed Ian Greaves, John Williams and David Rolinson. London, Oberon Books, 2015. ISBN 9781783192038.

Purser-Hallard, Philip, *Dark Water / Death in Heaven*. **The Black Archive** #4. Edinburgh, Obverse Books, 2016. ISBN 9781909031401.

Rowling, J K, *Harry Potter and the Goblet of Fire*. London, Bloomsbury Publishing, 2000. ISBN 9780747546245.

Russell, Gary, *Doctor Who: The Inside Story*. London, BBC Books, 2006. ISBN 9780563486497.

Segal, Philip, with Gary Russell, *Doctor Who: Regeneration*. London, HarperCollinsPublishers, 2000. ISBN 9780007105915.

Tribe, Steve, *Doctor Who: Companions and Allies*. London, BBC Books, 2009. ISBN 9781846077494.

Wilson, Carl, *Let's Talk About Love: Why Other People Have Such Bad Taste*. London, Bloomsbury Academic, 2007. ISBN 9781441166777.

Periodicals

Doctor Who Magazine (DWM). Marvel UK, Panini, BBC, 1979-.

'Doctor Who: The First 50 Years'. DWM #474, cover date July 2014

DWM Special Edition #24: *In Their Own Words Volume 6: 1997-2009*, cover date April 2010.

Cook, Benjamin, 'Brave New Worlds'. DWM #373, cover date September 2006.

Davies, Russell T, 'Production Notes #3: Coffee and TV'. DWM #343, cover date May 2004.

Davies, Russell T, 'Production Notes #4: Think of A Number'. DWM #344, cover date June 2004.

Davies, Russell T, 'A Long Game'. DWM #359, cover date August 2005.

Davies, Russell T, 'Tooth and Claw'. DWM #360, cover date September 2005.

Davies, Russell T, 'Pitch Perfect'. DWM Special Edition, *The Doctor Who Companion Series One*, cover date August 2005.

Pixley, Andrew, 'DWM Archive: Doctor Who – The Movie'. DWM Special Edition #5: *The Complete Eighth Doctor*, cover date July 2003.

Roberts, Gareth, 'Guess Who?'. *The Doctor Who Companion: Series One*, DWM Special Edition #11, July 2005.

Scott, Cavan, 'The Way Back Part One: Bring Me To Life'. DWM #463, cover date September 2013.

Various, 'We're Gonna Be Bigger Than Star Wars!'. DWM #279, cover date June 1999.

Bilmes, Alex, 'The stage was set. And we turned up. And the people said "Yes." And then it just exploded'. *Esquire*, December 2015.

Brook, Stephen, 'Carry on Doctor'. *The Guardian*, 9 March 2005.

O'Brien, Steve, and Nick Setchfield, 'Russell Spouts'. SFX Special Edition #20: *SFX Collection Doctor Who Past! Present! Future!*, 2005.

Venning, Harry, 'TV Review'. *The Stage*, 4 March 2005.

Television

The A-Team. Universal Television, Stephen J Cannell Productions, 1983-87.

The Adventures of Sir Lancelot. Sapphire Films, 1956-57.

Angels Are So Few. BBC, 1970.

Ant and Dec's Saturday Night Takeaway. LWT, Granada Productions, ITV Productions, Gallowgate, Mitre Television, 2002-.

The Avengers. Associated British Corporation, 1961-69.

Babylon 5. Babylonian Productions Ltd, Synthetic Worlds Ltd, 1993-1998.

Banana. Red Production Company, 2015.

Bella and the Boys. BBC, Century Films, 2004.

Big Brother. Endemol UK, 2000-.

Bob and Rose. Red Production Company, 2001.

Brimstone and Treacle. BBC, 1976.

Buffy the Vampire Slayer. Mutant Enemy Productions, 1997-2003.

The Canterbury Tales. BBC, 2003.

Casanova. BBC, 1971.

Casanova. Red Production Company, Powercorp, BBC Films, 2005.

Century Falls. BBC, 1993.

Children's Ward / The Ward. Granada Productions, 1989-2000.

ChuckleVision. BBC, 1987-2009.

Class. BBC, 2016.

Cracker. Granada Television, 1993-95, 1996, 2006.

Cucumber. Red Production Company, 2015.

Dark Season. BBC, 1991.

Dark Skies. Bryce Zabel Productions, Columbia Pictures Television, 1996-97.

Dixon of Dock Green. BBC, 1955-76.

Doctor Who. BBC, 1963-.

The Flashing Blade. ORTF, BBC, 1967, 1969, 1988.

Game of Thrones. HBO, 2011-.

The Grand. Granada Television, 1997-98.

Grandstand. BBC, 1958-2007.

The Hot Shoe Show. BBC, 1983-84.

Just William. LWT, 1977-78.

Knight Rider. Glen A Larson Productions, Universal Television, 1982-86.

Lois and Clark: The New Adventures of Superman. December 3rd Productions, Gangbuster Films Inc, Roundelay Productions, Warner Bros Television, 1993-97.

Mine All Mine. Red Production Company, 2004.

The National Lottery: Jet Set. BBC, 2001-07.

Newsnight Review (aka **The Late Review** and **The Review Show**). BBC, 1994-2014.

On the Waterfront. BBC, 1988-89.

The One That Got Away. LWT, 1996.

Our Friends in the North. BBC, 1996.

Roseanne. Wind Dancer Productions, Carsey-Werner Company, Paramount Television, 1988-97.

Revelations. Granada Television, 1994-96.

Safe House. Eleventh Hour Films, 2015-.

The Sarah Jane Adventures. BBC, 2007-11.

Son of Man. BBC, 1969.

Springhill. Granada Television, 1996-97.

Star Trek. Desilu Productions, Norway Corporation, Paramount Television, 1966-69.

Star Trek: Enterprise. Braga Productions, Paramount Network Television, Paramount Television, 2001-05.

Strictly Come Dancing. BBC, 2004-.

Strictly Dance Fever. BBC, 2005-06.

Target. BBC, 1977-78.

The Telegoons. BBC, 1963-64.

Torchwood. BBC Wales, BBC Worldwide, Canadian Broadcasting Corporation, Starz Entertainment, 2006-11.

The West Wing. John Wells Productions, Warner Bros Television, 1999-2006.

Why Don't You…?. BBC, 1973-95.

The X Factor. Syco Entertainment, Thames, Talkback Thames, 2004-

The X-Files. Ten Thirteen Productions, 20th Television, 20th Century Fox Television, 1993-2002, 2016.

Film

Myth Makers: Jon Pertwee. Reeltime Pictures, 1989.

Curtis, Richard, dir, *Love Actually*. Universal Pictures, Studio Canal, Working Title Films, 2003.

Donner, Richard, dir, *Superman The Movie*. Dovemead Films, Film Export A.G., International Film Production, 1978.

Farrelly, Peter, dir, *Dumb and Dumber*. Motion Picture Corporation of America, 1994.

Lucas, George, dir, *Star Wars: Episode IV – A New Hope*. Lucasfilm, Twentieth Century Fox, 1977.

Medak, Peter, dir, *Let Him Have It*. British Screen Productions, Canal+, Film Trustees Ltd, 1991.

Newell, Mike, dir, *Four Weddings and a Funeral*. Polygram Filmed Entertainment, Channel Four Films, Working Title Productions, 1994.

Weitz, Paul, dir, *American Pie*. Zide-Perry Productions, 1999.

Audio CD

Platt, Marc, *Thin Ice*. **Doctor Who: The Lost Stories**. Big Finish Productions, 2011.

Robson, Eddie, *Situation Vacant*. **Doctor Who: The Eighth Doctor Adventures**. Big Finish Productions, 2010.

Web

'Airdates in the UK (BBC Repeats)', BroaDWcast. http://gallifreybase.com/w/index.php/Airdates_in_the_UK_(BBC_r epeats). Accessed 6 December 2015.

'Big Brother: BB1 – Nick Gets Caught – Channel 4', YouTube. https://www.youtube.com/watch?v=ri01fflx. Accessed 6 December 2015.

'Doctor Who Returns to BBC One', BBC. http://www.bbc.co.uk/pressoffice/pressreleases/stories/2003/09_september/26/dr_who.shtml. Accessed 6 December 2015.

'Internet Users', Internet Live Stats. http://www.internetlivestats.com/internet-users/. Accessed 6 December 2015.

'Internet Access - Households and Individuals, 2014', Office for National Statistics. http://www.ons.gov.uk/ons/publications/re-reference-tables.html?edition=tcm%3A77-322080. Accessed 6 December 2015.

Bahn, Christopher, 'TV Club Interview: Russell T Davies'. *AV Club*, 27 July 2009. http://www.avclub.com/article/russell-t-davies-30869. Accessed 6 December 2015.

Ewing, Tom, 'Imperial'. *Pitchfork*, 28 May 2010. http://pitchfork.com/features/poptimist/7811-poptimist-29/. Accessed 6 December 2015.

Grieves, Robert T, 'Video: Who's Who in Outer Space'. *Time*, 9 January 1984. http://content.time.com/time/magazine/article/0,9171,952321-2,00.html (subscription required). Accessed 6 December 2015.

Morley, Christopher, 'Doctor Who: Stories From The Scrapheap – The New Team/Pompeii'. *Warped Factor*. http://www.warpedfactor.com/2014/10/doctor-who-stories-from-scrapheap-new.html. Accessed 6 December 2015.

Niven, Larry, 'Man of Steel, Woman of Kleenex'. http://www.rawbw.com/~svw/superman.html. Accessed 6 December 2015.

Sullivan, Shannon Patrick, 'Dragonfire', *A Brief History of Time (Travel)*. http://www.shannonsullivan.com/drwho/serials/7g.html. Accessed 6 December 2015.

Sunday People, 'Paul Daniels to Be Doctor Who', *Daily Mirror*, 8 February 2004. http://www.mirror.co.uk/news/world-news/paul-daniels-to-be-dr-who-1597288. Accessed 6 December 2015.

Vivarelli, Nick, 'Lucca Comics: Doctor Who Showrunner Steven Moffat on Why the Reboot Is a Global Hit'. *Variety*, 31 October 2015. http://variety.com/2015/tv/news/doctor-who-steven-moffat-lucca-comics-1201631032/. Accessed 4 December 2015.

Webber, C E, 'Concept Notes for New SF Drama'. Internal BBC memo, 29 March 1963. http://www.bbc.co.uk/archive/doctorwho/6402.shtml?page=1. Accessed 6 December 2015.

BIOGRAPHY

Jon Arnold is the co-editor of *Shooty Dog Thing: 2th and Claw*. He has contributed to ten essay collections including *Hating to Love* and *Outside In 2*, and to innumerable fanzines and websites such as *The Two Unfortunates* and *Winterwind*. His fiction has appeared in *Shelf Life*, *The Twelve Doctors of Christmas*, *Terrors of the Theatre Diabolique* and *Secret Invasion: Tales of Eldritch Horrors from the West Country*. He's also an occasional contributor to the Reality Bomb podcast.

He tweets as @The_Arn and blogs at http://equilateral-chainsaw.blogspot.co.uk/.